SEMPER FIDELIS

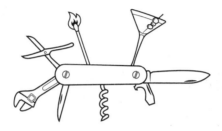

THE COMPLETE
WORST-CASE SCENARIO
Survival Handbook

MAN SKILLS

The
COMPLETE
WORST-CASE SCENARIO
Survival Handbook
MAN SKILLS

By Joshua Piven, David Borgenicht, and Ben H. Winters

With contributions by Victoria De Silverio, Jim Grace,
Sarah Jordan, Piers Marchant, Dan and Judy Ramsey,
Sam Stall, and Jennifer Worick

Illustrations by Brenda Brown

CHRONICLE BOOKS
SAN FRANCISCO

Worst-Case Scenario® and The Worst-Case Scenario Survival Hand-
book™ are trademarks of Quirk Productions, Inc.

Library of Congress Cataloging-in-Publication Data available.

ISBN: 978-0-8118-7483-0

Manufactured in Canada
Designed by Jenny Kraemer
Illustrations by Brenda Brown
Visit www.worstcasescenarios.com

10 9 8 7 6 5 4 3 2 1

Chronicle Books LLC
680 Second Street
San Francisco, CA 94107
www.chroniclebooks.com

WARNING

When a life is imperiled or a dire situation is at hand, safe alternatives may not exist. To deal with the worst-case scenarios presented in this book, we highly recommend—insist, actually—that the best course of action is to consult a professionally trained expert. But because highly trained professionals may not always be available when the safety or sanity of individuals is at risk, we have asked experts on various subjects to describe the techniques they might employ in these emergency situations. THE PUBLISHER, AUTHORS, AND EXPERTS DISCLAIM ANY LIABILITY from any injury that may result from the use, proper or improper, of the information contained in this book. All the answers in this book come from experts in the situation at hand, but we do not guarantee that the information contained herein is complete, safe, or accurate, nor should it be considered a substitute for your good judgment or common sense. And finally, nothing in this book should be construed or interpreted to infringe on the rights of other persons or to violate criminal statutes; we urge you to obey all laws and respect all rights, including property rights, of others.

—The Authors

CONTENTS

5 | **Work . . . 329**

No man is ever old enough to know better.

—Holbrook Jackson

INTRODUCTION

Being a man is a dangerous business. From the days of the Round Table, when chivalrous knights were always riding out to defend the honor of some maiden and ending up on the wrong end of a lance, we men have had our work cut out for us. The modern young gallant doesn't have it much easier: chained in his necktie and flat-front khaki trousers, he navigates a daily round of pitfalls, from nasty bosses to wicked sand traps to the searing flames leaping off the barbeque grill.

Then of course there's the greatest danger that man faces: woman. The presence of women in the lives of men causes no end of difficulties—from having to field questions like "Do I look fat in this?" to figuring out the best way to apologize when you don't exactly know what you've done wrong.

But women aren't really the main problem. The main thing that gets us men into dangerous situations is, well, ourselves. It's the belief, cherished in the heart of every man in the world—single and married, young and old—that he is James Bond. No amount of reality checking will convince a man that he is not, deep down, a dashing and glamorous super-genius involved in a series of top-secret adventures. And while most of us don't carry guns, we do have something in our pants that frequently gets us into foolhardy situations.

So, firm in his belief that he can handle any situation, the man puts way too much faith in his ability to, for example, find his way home without asking directions, or make a sandwich without looking up from the TV.

If you are a man, then you know you've heard yourself say these things:

Of course I know how to grill a steak.

Of course I can open a beer bottle without an opener.

Of course I can take that guy.

Now, at last, you really can do all those things you've always said you could. The book and accompanying DVD you now hold in your manly, hairy man hands will guide you through all the tests of manhood you can imagine, and plenty more besides.

In the pages that follow you will discover how to drive down a flight of stairs (page 61) and flatter an insecure boss (page 336). You'll learn how to find your way without a compass (page 433), survive a night in jail (page 494) and survive a pirate attack (page 44). You'll learn the right way to tie a tie, the smart way to handle a shaving accident, and a good way to spot fake boobs. And for those men who've entered into the most perilous situation of all—fatherhood—you'll learn how to use pacifiers, calm teenagers, and chase off monsters under the bed.

So soldier on, brave man! With *The Complete Worst-Case Scenario Survival Handbook: Man Skills*, you will be ready for whatever danger the world throws at you next. Also, the book is pretty thick, so if you hold it up right, it might just keep that lance from piercing your breastbone.

—The Authors

CHAPTER I

GREAT ESCAPES

HOW TO
CRASH-LAND
A PLANE ON WATER

These instructions apply to small passenger propeller planes (not commercial airliners).

1 Take your place at the controls.
If the plane has dual controls, the pilot will be in the left seat. Sit on the right. If the plane has only one set of controls and the pilot is unconscious, remove the pilot from the pilot's seat. Securely fasten your seat belt.

2 Put on the radio headset (if there is one) and call for help.
There will be a control button on the yoke (the plane's steering wheel) or a CB-like microphone on the instrument panel. Depress the button to talk, release it to listen. Say "Mayday! Mayday!" and give your situation, destination, and plane call numbers (which should be printed on the top of the instrument panel). If you get no response, try again on the emergency channel, 121.5. The person on the other end should be able to talk you through proper landing procedures. If you cannot reach someone to talk you through the landing process, you will have to do it alone.

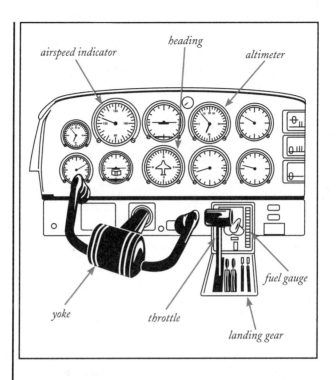

airspeed indicator

heading

altimeter

yoke

throttle

landing gear

fuel gauge

3 Get your bearings and identify the instruments.

YOKE. This is the steering wheel, and it should be in front of you. The yoke turns the plane and controls its pitch. Pull back on the column to bring the nose up, push forward to point it down. Turn it left to turn the plane left, turn it right to turn the plane right. The yoke is very sensitive—move it only an inch or two in either direction to turn the plane. While cruising, the nose of the plane should be about three inches below the horizon.

ALTIMETER. This is the most important instrument, at least initially. It is often a black-faced dial in the middle of the panel with white hands and numerals, with zero at the top. The small hand indicates feet above sea level in thousand-foot increments, the large hand in hundreds.

HEADING. This is a compass. It will be the only instrument with a small image of a plane in the center. The nose of the image will point in the direction the plane is headed.

AIRSPEED. This dial is on the top of the instrument panel and will be on the left. It is usually calibrated in knots, though it may also have miles per hour. A small plane travels at about 120 knots while cruising. Anything under 70 knots in the air is dangerously close to stall speed. (A knot is 1¼ mph.)

TACHOMETER. This instrument (not visible in ill., but located near the throttle) displays the engine's power in revolutions per minute (rpm). In more sophisticated aircraft, a manifold pressure gauge may be present. This gauge supplies manifold pressure in inches of mercury, and shows you how much power an engine is producing. If present, it should be used in place of the tachometer. (One inch of mercury equals approximately 100 rpm; 10 inches corresponds to 1,000 rpm.)

THROTTLE. This lever controls airspeed (power) and also the nose attitude, its relation to the horizon. It sits between the seats and is always black. Pull it toward you to slow the plane and cause it to descend, push it away from you to speed up the plane and cause it to ascend.

FUEL. The fuel gauges will be on the lower portion of the instrument panel. If the pilot has followed FAA regulations, the plane should have enough fuel for the amount of flying time to your intended destination, plus at least an additional half hour of reserve. Some planes have a reserve fuel tank in addition to the primary one, but do not attempt to change tanks. Full tanks will provide 4½ to 5 hours of flying time for a light aircraft. If the gauge indicates the tanks are half full, you will have half that time. However, be advised that fuel gauges on airplanes can be inexact and experienced pilots do not rely on them. Always assume you have a fuel emergency despite what the fuel gauge may indicate. You want to land the plane as soon as possible to avoid an uncontrolled landing.

MIXTURE CONTROL. This is a red knob or lever on the instrument panel, or between the pilot and copilot positions. The knob regulates fuel flow to the engine. Pull it out (toward you) to reduce fuel flow, push it in (away from you) to increase it.

AUTOPILOT. The autopilot panel will be on the lower third of the instrument panel and will generally be to the immediate left or right of the yoke. There will be an on/off switch and separate switches or buttons reading "alt," "heading," and "nav."

FLAPS. The flaps are the moveable parts of the wings that are used to change the speed of the plane and adjust its altitude. Due to their complexity, wing flaps can make the plane hard to control. Use the throttle to control airspeed instead.

4 If the plane is flying straight and level, engage the autopilot.

Press the "alt" (altitude) and heading buttons until the displays read "hold." This will maintain your present altitude and heading and give you an opportunity to continue to use the radio and assess your landing choices.

5 Once you have determined your landing strategy, turn the autopilot off and reduce power by moving the throttle toward you.

Slowly move the throttle enough to cause the nose to drop and the plane to descend slightly. You will need to be at approximately 2,000 feet to be able to clearly see the water below you.

6 When the altimeter reads 2,000 feet, level the nose with the horizon using the yoke.

Increase power slightly by moving the throttle away from you if pulling back on the yoke does not work.

7 Assess the water ahead of you.

It is imperative that you land in calm water and that you avoid landing the plane in the face of swells, where there is a significant risk of waves breaking over the aircraft. The plane should be heading into the wind (called a headwind), so you land on the backside of any waves.

8 Reduce power by moving the throttle toward you.

Do not use your flaps or your landing gear, which might catch on the water. Bring the plane to an altitude of 100 to 200 feet.

9 Continue to reduce power until the tachometer reads 1,500 to 1,700 rpm or 15 to 17 inches of mercury.

10 Move the nose of the plane up at least 5 to 10 degrees above the horizon by pulling the yoke toward you slightly.

You must exercise a nose-up landing to keep the propeller out of the water and prevent the plane from flipping end-over-end. The angle of the nose should be such that the horizon is almost completely obscured.

11 Just before touchdown, make sure the throttle is in its furthest position toward you.

The plane should be no more than 10 feet above the water at this point.

12 Pull the red fuel mixture control knob toward you to cut fuel to the engine when the plane is about five feet above the water.

Use the surface of the water, not the altimeter, to judge your altitude at this low level.

13 Keep the nose up by pulling back gently on the yoke. The plane should fall gently onto the water. Concentrate on making sure the rear of the plane hits the water first. If the plane has nonretractable landing gear, it will most likely flip over because the landing gear will catch on the water.

14 Open the door or window as soon as you hit the water, and quickly get out of the plane.

It may be difficult to open the door or window once you begin to sink. If you are unable to open the cabin door, kick out the windshield.

15 If the plane has life vests or a raft, inflate them outside of the plane.

The plane's emergency location transmitter (ELT) should continue broadcasting your location to rescue personnel.

HOW TO SURVIVE
AN AVALANCHE

1 Struggle to stay on top of the snow by using a free-style swimming motion.

2 If you are buried, your best chance of survival is if someone saw you get covered.

The snow in an avalanche is like a wet snowball: it is not light and powdery, and once you are buried, it is very difficult to dig your way out.

3 If you are only partially buried, you can dig your way out with your hands or by kicking at the snow.

If you still have a ski pole, poke through the snow in several directions until you see or feel open air, then dig in that direction.

4 If you are completely buried, chances are you will be too injured to help yourself.

However, if you are able, dig a small hole around you and spit in it. The saliva should head downhill, giving you an idea of which direction is up. Dig up, and do it quickly.

Be Aware
• Never go hiking or skiing alone in avalanche territory.
• Carry an avalanche probe—a sturdy, sectional aluminum pole that fits together to create a probe

*Struggle to stay on top of the snow by
using a freestyle swimming motion.*

six to eight feet in length. Some ski poles are
threaded and can be screwed together to form
avalanche probes.

* Know where and when avalanches are likely
  to occur.
* Avalanches occur in areas with new snow; on the
  leeward side of mountains (the side facing away
  from the wind); and in the afternoons of sunny
  days, when the morning sun may have loosened the
  snowpack. They occur most often on mountainsides
  with angles of 30 to 45 degrees—these are often the
  most popular slopes for skiing.

- Avalanches can be triggered by numerous factors, including recent snowfall, wind, and sunlight. As new snow accumulates with successive storms, the layers may be of different consistencies and not bond to one another, making the snow highly unstable.
- Loud noises do not cause avalanches except if they cause significant vibrations in the ground or snow.
- The activity with the highest avalanche risk is now snowmobiling. Snowmobiles—sometimes called mountain sleds—are powerful and light, and can get high into mountainous terrain, where avalanches occur.
- Carry a beacon. The beacon broadcasts your position by setting up a magnetic field that can be picked up by the other beacons in your group. If skiing on a dangerous slope, go down one at a time, not as a group, in case a slide occurs.

How to Rescue Others

If you have witnessed others being buried by an avalanche, contact the ski patrol as soon as possible. Then search first by trees and benches—the places where people are most commonly buried. All searchers should have small, collapsible shovels to help them dig quickly if they find someone.

how to survive an avalanche

HOW TO OUTWIT
A PACK OF WOLVES

1 Slowly move to solid terrain.

In winter, wolves tend to chase their prey into deep snow or onto frozen lakes, surfaces where the hooves of the victim sink or slide. The wolves' large, padded feet give them a tremendous range-of-movement advantage in these areas. If you see wolves around you, slowly walk toward solid ground. Do not crouch down, and do not run. Even during warmer months, wolves will readily chase prey over solid ground and are capable of bursts of high speed, as fast as 35 mph over short distances. You cannot outrun a wolf.

2 Observe the wolves' posture.

A wolf can attack from any position, but a tail straight up in the air and ears pricked up are a signal of dominance and often indicate that the wolf is preparing to attack.

3 Charge one member of the pack.

Wolves are generally timid around humans and have a strong flight response. Running toward one wolf while yelling may scare it and the other members of the pack away from you.

4 Throw sticks and rocks.

If the wolves continue with an attack, throw sticks and rocks at those closest to you. Wolves tend to attack the lower portions of their victims' bodies in an attempt to hobble and then bring them to the ground. Kick or hit the wolves as they approach your legs until you scare them off.

Be Aware

- Captive wolves are more likely to attack a human than wolves in the wild. Attacks are often a dominance display. Captive wolves may attack and then eat a person.
- Solitary wolves are generally considered more of an attack threat to humans than pack wolves, though a pack of wolves can inflict more damage more quickly.
- Wild wolves habituated to the presence of humans are more likely to attack, since they have lost their fear of people.
- Wolves may hunt at any hour of the day or night.
- The bite pressure of an adult wolf is about 1,500 pounds per square inch. By contrast, the bite pressure of a German shepherd is about 500 pounds per square inch.
- A wolf pack may have 30 members.

HOW TO ESCAPE
FROM FIRE ANTS

1 Brush the ants off.

Fire ants inject venom from a stinger connected to a poison gland. A single ant will pinch the skin with its jaws and sting numerous times, injecting more venom with each sting. As the venom enters the skin, you will experience the intense, burning sensation that gives fire ants their name. Using your hand or a cloth, make a fast, sharp, brushing motion until their jaws dislodge from the skin and they fall off. Jumping up and down, shaking the affected area, and placing the ants under running water will not prevent the ants from attacking and may cause further injury.

2 Run from the area.

As you remove the ants, flee the area of the attack. When a mound or nest is disturbed, or foraging fire ants are encountered, they immediately climb up any vertical surface and sting. Hundreds of ants may attack within seconds, especially in mild to high temperatures, when ants stay closer to the surface. The ants will continue to attack even after you have left the nest area, however. Continue brushing them as you run.

3 Remove your clothing.

Fire ants will stay in the creases of clothing and may sting later. Once you have reached safety and removed all visible ants, take off your shoes, socks, pants, and any other articles of clothing where the ants were visible. Inspect your clothes carefully, especially the pockets and seams, before putting them back on. If possible, launder the items before wearing them again.

4 Treat the affected area.

After several minutes, the site of each bite will redden and swell into a bump. A topical antihistamine may relieve some itching at bite sites. Several hours to several days later, the bumps will become white, fluid-filled pustules, which will last for several days or, in some cases, weeks. Immediately upon the appearance of pustules, treat the affected areas with a solution of half bleach, half water to lessen pain and reduce itching. Use an over-the-counter pain medication to reduce discomfort. Pustules will form regardless of topical treatment. If pustules break, treat with a topical antibacterial ointment to prevent infection. Pustules may leave scars.

5 Monitor symptoms.

Even a healthy adult may have a severe reaction to hundreds of stings, and people with certain allergies may develop serious complications. Watch for severe chest pain, nausea, severe sweating, loss of breath, severe swelling of limbs, and slurred speech. Seek immediate medical attention if any of these symptoms are present. In highly allergic people, anaphylaxis may occur from fire ant stings. Administer epinephrine immediately.

HOW TO TREAT A RAT BITE

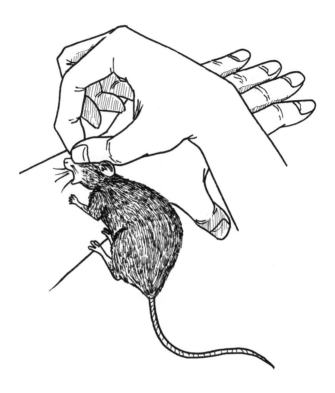

Remove the rat by pinching the upper jaw of the rat with your index finger and thumb. Stop any blood flow with pressure from a clean, dry cloth. Clean the bite and any other parts of your body that touched the rat with soap and water. Loosely apply a bandage or gauze to the wound.

HOW TO DEAL WITH A CHARGING BULL

1 Do not antagonize the bull, and do not move.
Bulls will generally leave humans alone unless they become angry.

2 Look around for a safe haven—an escape route, cover, or high ground.
Running away is not likely to help unless you find an open door, a fence to jump, or another safe haven—bulls can easily outrun humans. If you can reach a safe spot, make a run for it.

3 If a safe haven is not available, remove your shirt, hat, or another article of clothing.
Use this to distract the bull. It does not matter what color the clothing is. Despite the colors bullfighters traditionally use, bulls do not naturally head for red—they react to and move toward movement, not color.

4 If the bull charges, remain still and then throw your shirt or hat away from you.
The bull should head toward the object you've thrown.

If you cannot find safe cover from a charging bull, remove articles of clothing and throw them away from your body. The bull will veer and head toward the moving objects.

IF YOU ENCOUNTER A STAMPEDE

If you encounter a stampede of bulls or cattle, do not try to distract them. Try to determine where they are headed, and then get out of the way. If you cannot escape, your only option is to run alongside the stampede to avoid getting trampled. Bulls are not like horses, and will not avoid you if you lie down—so keep moving.

HOW TO FEND OFF
A VICIOUS DOG

1 Hide.
Take refuge in an unlocked car, tree, or other protected space. Do not attempt to seek safety unless you are certain you can make it.

2 Stand your ground.
When the dog approaches, do not run. It makes you look weak, or like prey.

3 Look tough.
Stand tall. Appear confident.

4 Sound tough.
Tell him "No," in a firm voice. Speak loudly but do not shout.

5 Do not make prolonged eye contact.

6 Back away slowly.
Dogs are highly territorial and will often lose interest once you leave their home base. Remain aware of the canine's whereabouts as you withdraw.

7 Defend yourself.
After the dog snarls and lunges, use sticks or hurl shoes to keep the dog out of biting range. If the dog hesitates, charge toward it and scream as loudly as

Take refuge in a tree.

possible. A sudden show of strength may end the encounter or it may antagonize the dog. Remain on your feet and out of biting range.

8 Divert the attack.
Remove your jacket and wrap it loosely around one of your arms. Hold the protected arm in front of you and make it an inviting and obvious target. When the dog latches onto your coat, quickly pull your arm free of the garment and flee.

9 Curl up.
If you stumble or the dog makes contact, roll your body into the fetal position. Use your hands to protect your throat and face. Do not get up until you are sure the dog has departed.

Be Aware

- Fleeing an attacking canine is both dangerous (it exposes your vulnerable back, buttocks, and calves to attack) and pointless (the top speed of a typical human is 15 mph; a dog can reach 45 mph).
- There is no such thing as a "minor" dog bite. What looks like a simple puncture wound may conceal muscle damage caused when the animal latched on and violently shook his head. Also, bites can lead to infection—even, possibly, to rabies. Seek medical attention no matter how minor the injuries may seem.

HOW TO SURVIVE A PIRATE ATTACK

1 Once pirates have been spotted, take evasive action.
In safe water conditions, change directions radically.
Increase speed, heading for the coast if possible.

2 Let others know.
Transmit a danger message to ships in the vicinity.
Raise a distress signal on VHF channel 16 stating your
position—the effectiveness of assistance by shore-
based security forces depends on an early alarm.

3 Seal off access to the ship.
Attach rat guards to mooring lines and lock doors and
hatches.

4 Use water as a defensive tactic.
Spray water all over the deck to make it slippery, especially in areas where it is easiest for attackers to board.
Keep constant pressure in water hoses and consider
using them to repel attackers.

5 Use light and sound to confuse the raiders.
Shine lights into the eyes of pirates to blind them
as they scale the sides of your ship. Sound the alarm
and use intermittent blasts of the horn and rocket
signals to attract assistance from other ships. If necessary to protect the lives of crew members, fire signaling

Douse deck with water to make floor slick.

rockets into the pirates' access areas. Try to maintain control of navigation without endangering life.

6 If your vessel is boarded, cooperate.
Allow the pirates to take what they want, minimizing the time they spend on board. Resist the urge to commit heroic acts—the faster the pirates leave, the safer you will be. Do not threaten to use firearms, which may provoke violent action from pirates with superior weaponry.

7 Inform the authorities of the raid.
File a comprehensive report with the nearest Rescue Coordination Center. Notify the nearest coastal nation, as well as your ship's owners and flag state. Cooperate with subsequent investigation to help prevent future attacks.

How to Avoid a Pirate Attack

⭐ Look busy.
The majority of attacks will be deterred if pirates are aware that they have been observed. Instruct crew members to move constantly around the ship, signaling to potential attackers that the crew is alert and prepared.

⭐ Switch up your routine.
Make random rather than predictably timed patrols, preventing pirates from learning the ship's schedule.

★ **Strengthen night watches.**
Increase the number of crew members on guard, especially at the stern between the hours of 0100 and 0600, when most pirate attacks occur.

★ **Stay in constant radio contact with shore authorities and nearby vessels.**
When passing through pirate-infested waters, maintain a 24-hour watch and establish walkie-talkie contact between lookouts and the bridge.

★ **Make your vessel an unappealing quarry.**
Remove valuable items from the deck, and use overside and deck lights to illuminate the water and ward off potential raiders.

★ **Do not engage locals who approach your boat in small craft.**
What seems like an innocent attempt at trade may actually be a scouting mission for pirates.

Be Aware

Modern pirates are most prevalent in the waters of Southeast Asia and the Far East, especially near Indonesia and Malaysia. Pirates also frequent the coasts of Brazil and Ecuador in South America, the Bay of Bengal and the Somali coast in the Indian Ocean, and the area around Nigeria in the Atlantic.

HOW TO LOSE SOMEONE WHO IS FOLLOWING YOU

If You Are in a Car

1 Determine if you are actually being followed.
If you suspect a tail, observe the car as you continue to drive. If the car remains behind you, make three to four turns in a row to see if it continues to follow you. Then signal a turn in one direction but turn quickly in the other direction. See if the other car turns as well.

2 Once you are certain you are being followed, get on a highway, or drive to a populous and active area.
Do not drive home, to a deserted place, or down an alley. You are more likely to shake your tail in a crowd than in a deserted area.

3 Drive at the speed limit, or a bit slower.
Soon, another car (not that of your pursuer) will attempt to pass you. Speed up slightly so the car pulls in behind you. Repeat, but don't go so slowly that an innocent car behind you is able to pass you.

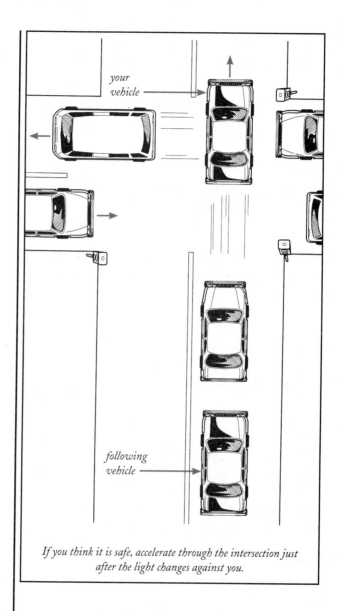

your vehicle

following vehicle

If you think it is safe, accelerate through the intersection just after the light changes against you.

4 | Slow down at a busy intersection with a traffic light, then accelerate through the intersection just after the light changes.

The car following you may get stuck at the red light. If you attract the attention of the police for running a red light, your pursuer will most likely leave the scene.

5 | When you have several cars around you, speed up, get off the highway (if you are on one), and make several quick turns to further elude your pursuer.

Your pursuer should be too far back to follow closely.

6 | Once you are out of sight of your pursuer, pull into a parking lot, a garage, or a shopping center with lots of other cars.

7 | If you still have not lost your tail at this point, drive to a police station and get help.

IF YOU ARE ON FOOT

1 | Determine if you are being followed, and identify your tail.

Take a random path: Make unexpected changes in direction at intersections and retrace your steps, effectively making a U-turn. Do not, however, get yourself disoriented or lost. Note any identifying characteristics of your tail (dress, gait, height, and weight).

2 | Keep an eye on your pursuer, but do not look back at him/her.

Use reflective surfaces such as shop windows to see behind you. If you have a makeup case with a mirror, use that.

3 Stay in crowds.
Do not head for home, to a deserted place, or down alleys.

4 Once you are certain that you are being followed, use these methods to shake your tail:
- Enter the front of a store, shop, or restaurant and go out through the back entrance—most restaurants have exits in the kitchen.
- Buy a ticket for a movie, enter after it has started, and leave through an emergency exit before your pursuer enters the theater.
- Use mass transit, and exit or enter the train or bus just before the doors close.

5 If you have not shaken your tail, walk to a police station or call the police from a public place.
Never head for home unless you are certain you are no longer being followed.

Be Aware
If you are certain your tail is not dangerous, you may want to confront your pursuer in a public place with many people around. Say that you know you are being followed and ask your pursuer why. Use this method only if you feel the person is not dangerous.

HOW TO
HOT-WIRE A CAR

Hot-wiring a car without the owner's permission is illegal, except in repossessions. Hot-wiring can be dangerous; there is a risk of electrical shock. Hot-wiring will not work on all cars, particularly cars with security devices. Some "kill switches" can prevent hot-wiring.

1 Open the hood.

2 Locate the coil wire (it is red).
To find it, follow the plug wires, which lead to the coil wire. The plug and coil wires are located at the rear of the engine on most V-8s. On six-cylinder engines, the wires are on the left side near the center of the engine, and on four-cylinder engines, they are located on the right side near the center of the engine.

3 Run a wire from the positive (+) side of the battery to the positive side of the coil, or the red wire that goes to the coil.
This step gives power to the dash, and the car will not run unless it is performed first.

4 Locate the starter solenoid.
On most GM cars, it is on the starter. On Fords, it is located on the left-side (passenger-side) fender well. An easy way to find it is to follow the positive battery cable. You will see a small wire and the positive

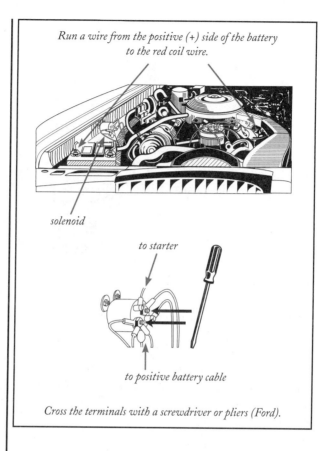

Run a wire from the positive (+) side of the battery
to the red coil wire.

solenoid

to starter

to positive battery cable

Cross the terminals with a screwdriver or pliers (Ford).

battery cable. Cross the two with a screwdriver or pliers.
This cranks the engine.

5 If the car has a standard transmission, make sure it
is in neutral and the parking brake is on.
If it has an automatic transmission, make sure it is
in park.

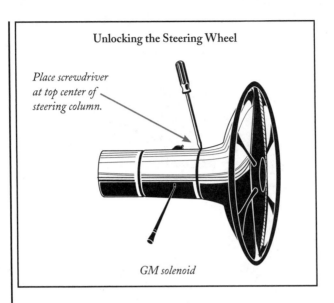

Unlocking the Steering Wheel

Place screwdriver at top center of steering column.

GM solenoid

6 Unlock the steering wheel using a flat blade screwdriver.

Take the screwdriver and place it at the top center of the steering column. Push the screwdriver between the steering wheel and the column. Push the locking pin away from the wheel. Be very firm when pushing the pin; it will not break.

How to Deal with a Fire Under the Hood

Pull over and turn off the engine. Do not open the hood. Exit the car and move at least 100 yards from the vehicle.

HOW TO JUMP FROM A MOVING CAR

Hurling yourself from a moving car should be a last resort; for example, if your brakes are defective and your car is about to head off a cliff or into a train.

1 Apply the emergency brake.
This may not stop the car, but it might slow it down enough to make jumping safer.

2 Open the car door.

3 Make sure you jump at an angle that will take you out of the path of the car.
Since your body will be moving at the same velocity as the car, you're going to continue to move in the direction the car is moving. If the car is going straight, try to jump at an angle that will take you away from it.

4 Tuck in your head and your arms and legs.

5 Aim for a soft landing site: grass, brush, wood chips, anything but pavement—or a tree.
Stuntpeople wear pads and land in sandpits. You won't have this luxury, but anything that gives a bit when the body hits it will minimize injury.

6 Roll when you hit the ground.

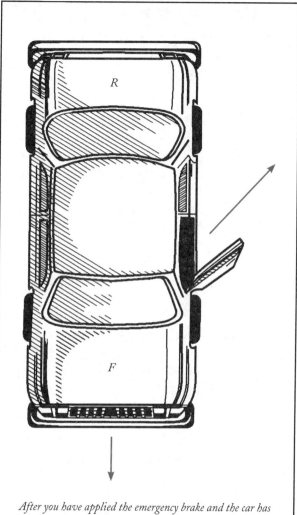

After you have applied the emergency brake and the car has slowed, open the car door. Jump out at an angle away from the direction in which the car is traveling.

HOW TO LEAP FROM A MOTORCYCLE TO A CAR

If you are planning to enter the car through one of its windows, remember that in many newer cars, only the front windows roll all the way down. You should attempt to be on the front passenger side.

1 Wear a high-quality helmet and a leather jacket plus leather pants and boots.

2 Make sure both vehicles are moving at the same speed. The slower the speed, the safer the move. Anything faster than 60 mph is extremely dangerous.

3 Wait for a long straight section of road.

4 Get the vehicles as close as possible to each other. You will be on the passenger side of the car, so you will be very close to the edge of the roadway. Be careful not to swerve.

5 Stand crouched with both of your feet on either the running board or the seat.

6 Hold the throttle until the last instant. Remember, as soon as you release the throttle the bike speed will decrease.

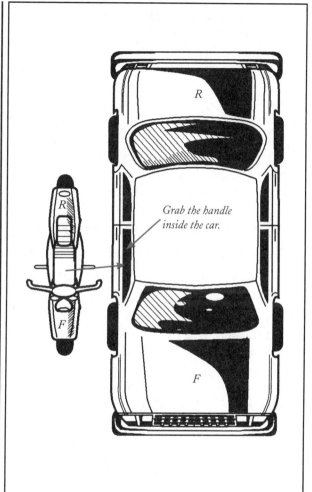

Grab the handle inside the car.

Attempt to leap into the front passenger window. Make sure the window is rolled down all the way, and move at the same speed as the car. Get as close as possible.

7 If the car has a handle inside (above the door) grab it with your free hand.

If not, simply time the leap so your torso lands in the car. If someone can grab you and pull you in, all the better.

8 Have the driver swerve away from the bike as soon as you are inside.

Once you have released the handlebars, the bike will go out of control and crash. It may also slip under the rear passenger-side wheel of the car.

9 If you miss the window, tuck and roll away from the vehicles.

Be Aware

The move is much easier if two people are on the motorcycle so that the nonjumper can continue driving. In the movies and in stunt shows, these transfers are usually performed at slow speeds, in fact, and often employ the use of a metal step installed on one side of the bike or car, which allows the rider to step off while keeping the bike balanced. You are not likely to have this option.

HOW TO DRIVE DOWN A FLIGHT OF STAIRS

1 Aim.
Set your eyes on a spot dead center over the horizon of the staircase, and steer the car at it.

2 Floor it.
When you are 20 feet from the stairs, slam your foot down on the accelerator to get a burst of speed approaching the lip.

3 Shut your mouth.
Pull your tongue back in your mouth and grit your teeth to keep them from knocking together as the car bounces down the stairs.

4 Grip the wheel.
Hold onto the wheel tightly, and steer to counterbalance each time the car jerks one way or the other as it bounces forward.

5 Lift your foot from the accelerator.
As the front bumper crosses the lip of the top stair, lift up your feet. Further acceleration is unnecessary as gravity pulls your vehicle forward, and leaving your feet on the pedals will cause your shins to absorb the shock as the car bangs down the steps.

Floor it when you feel the back wheel hit the bottom stair.

6 | Floor it again.
When you feel the back wheel hit the bottom stair, bring your right foot back down on the pedal and give another burst of speed to keep your back bumper from catching on the lip of the bottom step.

7 | Even out.
Hold tightly to the wheel and steer to regain control of the vehicle.

How to Drive Up a Flight of Stairs

1 | Aim and accelerate.
Check both side mirrors to make sure you are giving adequate space on either side. When you are 20 feet from the bottom stair, give a burst of gas.

2 | Further accelerate as your front wheel hits the first stair.
Give more gas to take your back wheels up onto the stairs.

3 | Maintain speed as you climb.
Continue to accelerate as you go up the stairs, to keep gravity from pulling you back down. Give a final burst of speed as you come over the top.

Be Aware
• If your car is too low to the ground, the underside will be scraped and banged by the stairs all the way

up or down, causing serious damage. Fully inflated tires will give you more clearance.

- Time permitting, laying down a wooden ramp across the bottom stair will make your approach to the uphill drive easier, and mitigate the effects of low clearance.
- A front-wheel drive car will be more effective than a rear-wheel drive car, while an all-wheel drive car is ideal, since the drive system sends more traction to the various tires as needed.

HOW TO RAM
A BARRICADE

1 Identify the barricade's weakest point.
The side of the barricade or gate that opens, or the place where a lock holds it closed, is usually its most vulnerable spot. Some barricades and gates have no locks at all: these are opened and closed by the force of an electric motor or magnet, which can be overpowered rather then rammed (see page 66).

2 Aim for the weak spot.
If possible, use the rear of the car to ram the weak spot—hitting with the front may damage the engine and cause the car to stall.

3 Accelerate to a speed of 30 to 45 mph.
Too rapid an approach will cause unnecessary damage to the car. Keep your foot on the gas all the way through. Consider how much room you will need to turn or stop once you clear the barricade.

4 Duck just before impact if you are heading toward an extremely tall barricade or fence.
Pieces of the barricade may come through your window or the windshield may shatter.

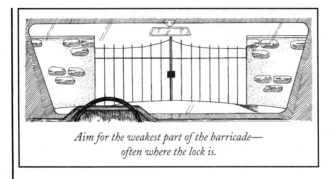

Aim for the weakest part of the barricade—
often where the lock is.

5 Avoid poles or anchors that are sunk into
the ground.
These may bend and not break, and then drag against
and damage the underside of the car, preventing you
from driving.

6 Repeat as necessary to break through.

ELECTRONIC GATES

Electrically powered gates that swing open and closed
(like those found in gated communities and apartment
complexes) are best pushed open rather than rammed.
Pushing or forcing the gate open with your car will
result in minimal damage and will almost always open
the gate. If you are traveling in the direction the gate
opens, simply ease your bumper up to the gate and
push. Your car will easily overpower the small electric
motor that operates the gate.

HOW TO SURVIVE IF YOUR CAR CAREENS DOWN A MOUNTAINSIDE

1 Apply firm and steady braking pressure.
Do not slam on the brakes as you leave the roadway and begin traveling down the slope. If you lock up your brakes, the wheels lose traction and may cause the vehicle to skid sideways, increasing the risk of a rollover.

2 Maintain a firm grip on the steering wheel.
The car is likely to bounce wildly and severely jostle you in your seat. Place your hands at the 10 and 2 o'clock positions. Keep your thumbs outside the steering wheel: If the car hits an object, the force may yank the steering wheel around, injuring your thumbs or arms.

3 Point the car downhill.
Keep the car facing and traveling straight downhill, continuing to apply steady braking pressure. A vehicle is much more likely to roll over if it is sideways across a hill. Though you may be able to survive a rollover, you will have no control and will not be able to stop the car.

4 Steer.
Keep the front wheels turned in the direction the car is sliding/moving in order to increase traction and make braking and steering more effective.

5 Downshift.
Once you regain control of the car and it is facing downhill, use engine braking to slow the car's momentum. If the car has a manual transmission, keep your foot off the gas and downshift to first gear. For an automatic, keep your foot off the gas and shift the car from drive to first gear or the lowest gear available. Continue to apply just enough braking pressure to control your speed, but not enough to lock up your wheels.

6 Turn the wheel in the same direction the car is sliding to regain control.
On a steep downslope, the weight of the car will transfer to the front axle as you brake, possibly causing the tail to spin out and around toward the front. To regain traction, turn the wheel in the direction the vehicle is sliding, then apply the gas lightly.

7 Use steady braking pressure to stop the car.
Once the car has stopped moving, apply the emergency brake and get out. If you cannot stop the car using the brakes, go to step 8.

Ram an obstacle only as a last resort.

8 Attempt to "high-center" the car.

If you are not able to stop the car in time to avoid an approaching cliff, look for a large rock or fallen tree. Drive over the object centered between your front wheels to try to force the car to "bottom out" and get stuck before the rear wheels roll over the obstacle. This maneuver will typically work only with an obstacle that is about one foot high. If you cannot high-center the car, continue to the next step.

9 Ram an obstacle.

Slow the car to 20 mph or less to increase your chance of survival. Ram the car head on into a tree or large boulder to stop your progress. Do not turn the car across the slope and ram the object sideways; you risk a rollover. You (and all passengers) must be wearing a seat belt and the car must have an air bag for you and your front-seat passenger. Ram the obstacle only as a last resort.

Be Aware

A vehicle's antilock braking system is usually not effective off-road: ABSs monitor wheel speed, and will apply the brakes only enough to equalize the rotation of the wheels, not to stop them from spinning when there is no traction. You will need to pump the brakes and to be aware that the braking system might apply pressure unequally to the wheels.

How to Get the Car Back to the Road

1 Assess damage to vehicle.
Once you have stopped the car, get out and inspect the vehicle. Check for brake fluid (red liquid pooling under the car) or damaged steering components (broken rods hanging down from the insides of the front wheels). Do not drive the car if it has a broken axle or damaged steering components, or if it is leaking brake fluid.

2 Walk your intended route before driving it.
Look for ditches, obstacles, and cliffs that may prevent you from getting back to the roadway.

3 | Drive slowly.
Use light acceleration and braking and smooth steering. Keep your speed to 5 mph or less, terrain permitting. Follow the off-roading maxim: "As slow as you can, as fast as you must."

4 | Monitor the path in front of you.
Look downslope to determine where you are headed and when you will need to stop the car. On a mountainside, the car will require 10 to 20 times its normal dry-pavement stopping distance.

5 | Look for a switchback.
Most steep mountain roads contain numerous switchbacks, or sharp turns that take you across the slope but at a slightly higher or lower elevation (depending on your direction of travel). If you see a lower section of the road cutting across the mountainside ahead of you, attempt to steer the car back onto the asphalt at the next opportunity. Watch for steep drop-offs that are common in mountain road cuts, however.

Be Aware

- Most passenger cars will roll side over side on any slope greater than 30 degrees.
- When your air bag deploys, fuel to the engine will likely be cut off, making further controlled driving impossible.

HOW TO SURVIVE
A ROLLOVER

1 Pull your feet off the pedals.
As the car starts to roll, lift your feet from the brake
and accelerator pedals and tuck them under the seat
to keep your ankles from breaking against the floor of
the vehicle.

2 Let go of the wheel.
If you are hanging onto the wheel when the car slams
into the ground again, the impact will be transmitted
through your entire body. Once the car has begun to
roll, turning the wheel will not have any effect.

3 Cross your arms over your chest.
Keep your arms and hands as far as possible from the windows of the car as the window side slams into the ground.

4 Brace yourself with your feet.
Once the car is upside down, find purchase somewhere
with both feet, either on the windshield, the driver's
side window, or on the ceiling of the car.

5 Count to sixty.
Remain still and suspended from your seatbelt until you
are certain that your vehicle has stopped moving, and
that any other vehicles involved in the accident have
stopped moving and are not sliding across the roadway
into yours.

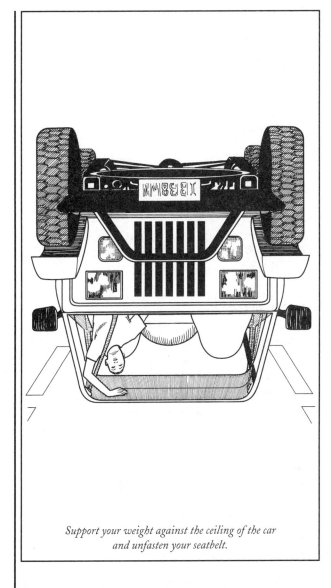

Support your weight against the ceiling of the car
and unfasten your seatbelt.

6 | Check yourself for injuries.
While hanging onto the seatbelt with one hand, pat your body with the other hand to check for injuries. Run your hand through your hair and over scalp. In case of any injury, do not move.

7 | If you appear to be uninjured, reach up and stabilize yourself.
As you are dangling from the seatbelt, slowly bring one hand up and lay it firmly against the ceiling of the car.

8 | Unfasten your seatbelt.
When you are certain your weight is fully supported by your hands and feet, unclick your seatbelt and drop down onto the ceiling.

9 | Escape from the car.
The vehicle's steel safety cage and roll bars may have preserved the integrity of the car, keeping the doors in working condition. If you cannot open the door, crawl through the window. If the window has not been broken during the rollover and is intact, try to roll it down. If you are unable to do so, use a metal object such as a steering wheel lock to break the glass.

10 | Run.
Move away from the car as quickly as possible in case there is a fuel leak, which could cause an explosion.

Be Aware

- Rollovers occur when a driver loses control of the vehicle, it slides sideways, and hits a "trip," such as a curb or guardrail. A second common cause is a driver taking a turn or curve too quickly.
- Rollovers account for only three percent of total accidents, but cause about a quarter of fatal crashes. More than half the people killed in single-vehicle crashes die in rollovers.
- Many rollover injuries occur after the accident itself, when the victim unbuckles his seatbelt and falls to the roof of the car.
- Rollovers are more common in pickup trucks than cars—mostly in SUVs, defined as passenger vehicles with high ground clearance (generally eight inches or higher) and with the same platform as a truck.
- Always wear your seatbelt.

HOW TO PEE IN THE CAR WHILE STUCK IN TRAFFIC

1 Cover the seat.

Arching your back to elevate your butt from the seat, completely cover the front seat of the car with paper towels or newspaper.

2 Find a container.

Look around the interior of the car for a cup with an open or resealable top, such as a travel mug, to-go cup, or refillable sports bottle. Widen the top of a plastic water bottle with a pocket knife or scissors. Avoid containers with small openings, such as glass bottles or aluminum cans.

3 Empty the container.

Roll down the window and dump the contents of the container outside of the car, careful not to splash adjacent vehicles or passersby, or damage the paint on your car.

4 Pull down your pants.

Keeping one hand on the wheel, reach down with your other hand, unbutton, unfasten, or adjust your clothing just enough to expose your nether regions.

5 Cradle the container between your legs.
Angle the opening of the container forward at a 45 degree angle.

6 Aim into the top of the container.
Cover your private parts, and the container, with a sweater or roadmap.

Keep your eyes on the road and maintain a neutral expression.

7 Do your business.
While you are urinating, keep your eyes fixed on the road and maintain a neutral facial expression. If you have passengers, turn up the radio to hide the noise of the stream.

8 Readjust your clothing.
Set the container in the car's cup-holder and refasten and readjust your clothing as normal.

9 Dump out the contents of the container
Roll down the window and dump the contents of the container outside of the car, being careful not to splash adjacent vehicles or passersby, or damage the paint on your car.

Be Aware
Holding in your urine for extended periods can put you at risk for urinary tract infections, and can distend your bladder, leading to an increased urinary frequency in the future.

HOW TO SURVIVE A BLOW-OUT ON THE ICE ROAD

1 Ride with your hand on the door.

The first sign of a blow-out—a wave of water under the ice that causes a tear in its surface—will be black water seeping through the ice's surface. If black water is visible, move one hand from the steering wheel to the handle of the door.

2 Speed up.

Ignore the instinct to brake, which can send the truck into a skid or exacerbate the blow-out by concentrating your weight on the crack. Accelerate by a few miles per hour to carry your weight forward past the crack.

3 Jump out.

When the front end of the truck starts to go through the ice, open the door of the cab and leap out.

4 Roll.

Upon landing, roll as quickly and as far as possible from the sinking cab.

5 Stay put.

Do not wander through the whiteout conditions in search of help, as you can quickly become disoriented. Stay where you are until another vehicle from your convoy can reach you.

Jump out of the cab as it falls through the ice.

Avoid a Blow-Out

1 Go slow.
Stay below 15 mph to avoid churning up the under-ice waves that lead to blow-outs.

2 Do not stop.
Keep your vehicle moving at all times, as the concentrated heat and weight of a stopped truck can cause the surface of the ice to crack.

3 | Know where the other drivers are.

Stay in radio and visual contact with the other members of your convoy to avoid a truck-on-truck collision, which will severely damage the ice floor.

Be Aware

- The ice roads, which can only be driven in the winter when the ice is sufficiently thick, cross the frozen lakes of Canada's Northwest Territories, servicing Canada's diamond mines.
- Until the ice is 42 inches thick, which usually happens in mid-February, the ice road cannot reliably bear the 70-ton weight of a fully loaded truck.
- The ice is most fragile closest to the shoreline.
- The sound of ice cracking beneath your rig is not alarming; frozen sheets of ice are constantly breaking and reforming to adjust to weight. If you don't hear cracking, the ice is too thin.

HOW TO SAVE YOURSELF IF YOU ARE HAVING A HEART ATTACK

1 Chew aspirin.

As soon as you suspect a heart attack, thoroughly chew and swallow one 325-mg aspirin tablet, or four 81-mg baby aspirins. For best effect, do not swallow the aspirin whole. Heart attacks occur when the blood vessels supplying oxygen to the heart muscle become clogged. Aspirin will not stop the heart attack or remove the blockage, but it will prevent blood clotting cells (platelets) from adding to the blockage.

2 Alert others.

If possible, tell people around you that you are having a heart attack. Instruct them to call emergency services.

3 Decrease the heart's oxygen consumption.

Stop all activity. The faster your heart pumps, the more oxygen it uses up. Think calming thoughts about bringing your heart rate down to one beat per second. If you have a watch with a second hand, focus on the second hand. For each second think or say quietly "heart-beat." Repeat.

4 | Increase oxygen delivery to the heart.
Lie down on the ground. Elevate your legs to keep as much blood pooled around your heart as possible; this will decrease the work your heart must do to pump blood. Open the windows to increase the room's oxygen level. If you have access to an oxygen tank, place the nasal cannula under your nose, turn the knob to four liters (or until you feel air coming through the nasal prongs), and take deep, slow breaths through your nose and out your mouth.

5 | Perform cough-CPR.
Breathe, then cough every three seconds. Take a breath in through your nose, think "heart-beat, heart-beat, heart-beat," then cough. Repeat. Coughing will deter fainting and help you stay conscious until conventional CPR can be administered.

Be Aware
Do not consume food or water. You may need a hospital procedure to "unclog" your arteries, and food or liquids in your system complicate treatment.

CHAPTER 2

SPORTS AND HOBBIES

HOW TO SKI OFF A 100-FOOT DROP

1 Look for danger below.
Just before you ski off the edge of the cliff, look down and out over the slope. If your projected path takes you toward rocks, trees, or another cliff, change your takeoff angle by jumping to the left or right so you will head toward safer, wide-open terrain.

2 Jump up and off the ledge.
Just as you are leaving the ground, hop up and slightly forward to help you clear any rocks or other obstructions that may be hidden just below the ledge and that could knock you off balance.

3 Pull your legs and skis up and tuck them under your rear end.
This compressed "ball" position will help you maintain balance while airborne and help you to land safely.

4 Thrust both arms out in front of you, elbows slightly bent.
Avoid the "cat out the window" position, where your arms and hands are splayed out above your head. That position will put you off balance when you land.

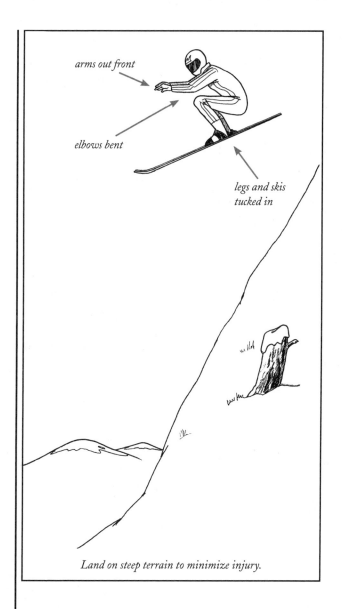

arms out front

elbows bent

legs and skis tucked in

Land on steep terrain to minimize injury.

5 Look out, not down.

Looking down at the ground will lead to a "door hinge" landing, where you bend forward at the waist and plant your face in the slope. Look out over the mountain.

6 Focus on a suitable landing site.

Land on very steep terrain. Avoid a low-angled slope or, worse, a flat section of the mountain. As long as the snow is powder and at least one foot deep, you should be able to land without serious injury.

7 Bend your knees as you land.

As you approach the side of the mountain, keep your knees bent to absorb the force of the impact with the ground. Avoid leaning back, which will cause a "tail first" landing and probable back injury. If you cannot ski away from a landing, land on your hip. Do not lean too far forward or you will fall on your face.

8 Extend your feet, bend your knees, and turn across (or "into") the mountain to slow down.

Because of your extreme speed while airborne, you must minimize acceleration by turning as soon as you land, or you risk hurtling down the mountain out of control. Modern skis should stay on top of deep powder instead of sinking, giving you a reasonable amount of control.

9 Continue making turns to keep control and reduce speed as you ski away.

Be Aware

- If you feel yourself falling backward while airborne, move your hands further in front of you and make fast circular motions, forward and back. This balancing maneuver is called "rolling down the windows."
- In any jump greater than 15 feet, avoid landing in the same spot a previous jumper landed; the snow will already be compacted and will not provide sufficient cushioning.

HOW TO SURVIVE A BUNGEE JUMPING DISASTER

The bungee cord is under maximum stress at the very bottom of your jump, before you rebound; it is at this point that a break is most likely. If you are over water and the cord breaks or comes loose, you will be falling head first and have about two seconds to prepare for impact.

1 Straighten your legs and body.
Put your feet and legs together, and point your toes.

2 Tuck your chin into your chest as far as it will go.
Avoid the urge to look at the water rushing up to meet you: It will result in black eyes, whiplash, or severe spinal trauma.

3 Point your arms below your head in a diving position.
Ball your fists.

4 Enter the water fists first.
Your hands will break the surface tension of the water, putting less stress on your head. If the bungee cord was attached and broke at your rebound point, it will have slowed you almost to a stop, making for a relatively safe entry. If the cord was not attached or came loose during your fall, the impact will be more severe.

Enter the water fists first.

how to survive a bungee jumping disaster

5 | Spread your arms and legs.
After entering the water, spread your arms and legs to slow your momentum and reduce the possibility of hitting the bottom.

6 | Swim to the surface.
Signal to the crew above that you are okay.

Be Aware

- Do not attempt to retie or hold the cord. You will not have time to tie a knot sufficient to support your weight, and the cord will fly out of your hands no matter how tightly you grasp it.
- Improper cord connection is a major source of bungee accidents. Before jumping, double-check that you are connected to the cord (generally with a carabiner) and the cord is connected to the bungee platform.
- Bungee cords are weight-specific, and you should always jump on a cord designed for your weight. Always overestimate, not underestimate, your weight.

HOW TO SURVIVE A RACE CAR SPINOUT

On the racetrack, a high-speed (180 mph or more) spinout is a rear-wheel skid or slide, also called "oversteer." To counteract oversteer and regain control of the car, take the following steps.

1 Turn into the spinout.
Determine which way the rear of the car is sliding, then turn the steering wheel in the same direction. For example, if the back of the car is sliding to the right, turn the steering wheel to the right. Do not jerk the wheel. Apply smooth, controlled inputs or you risk losing control. (The steering systems on race cars vary, but typical stock cars have power-assisted steering.)

2 Apply steady throttle.
Oversteer occurs when the rear wheels lose traction. Because most race cars are rear-wheel driven, stepping on the gas and accelerating transfers the car's weight to the rear wheels, aiding traction. (These same forces "push" you back into the driver's seat when you accelerate quickly during everyday driving; this is called "weight transfer.")

3 Do not brake.
Applying the brakes transfers weight to the front wheels, which will only increase your spin.

Steer in the same direction as the skid.

4 Focus on the track ahead of you.

During the skid (and after you regain control), make sure the car is heading in the proper direction. Observe the cars around you and concentrate on where you want the car headed, not where it is going.

5 Unwind the wheel.

As you feel the rear of the car begin to come in line, slowly bring the steering wheel back to center. Avoid attempting to "counteract" the spin by turning the wheel too far in the opposite direction. If you cannot regain control, continue to the next step.

6 │ Brake.

Once the car is out of control and a crash is imminent, apply the brakes to slow your rotational momentum.

7 │ Prepare for impact.

A stock car has a full race cage, a racing harness (a five-point seat belt), and a collapsible steering column, and you will be wearing a head and neck restraint. If you sense that impact with the wall or another vehicle is imminent, relax your body and let the car's safety devices protect you. Loosen your grip on the wheel or let go of it, keep your knees slightly bent, and do not tense your neck muscles.

8 │ Get out.

Your fire-protection suit and gloves are designed to protect you from heat and flames for several minutes. However, in the event of fire, get out of the car (climb through the window opening) as soon as it is safe to do so, or when help arrives.

Be Aware

- Do not downshift during a spinout—it is likely to lock the rear wheels. Downshift only when the car is moving in a straight line.
- Stock cars do not have air bags.
- All stock cars have braided, stainless-steel fuel lines to reduce the possibility of a fuel spill after a crash.
- The fuel tank in a stock car contains a rubber "bladder" filled with foam to absorb crash impact forces and reduce the chance of explosion.

- Standard racing tires (or "racing slicks") have no treads. The fewer the grooves, the more rubber the tire has against the road to increase traction. After multiple laps (the number varies with the tire compound and track conditions) tires get too hot, their rubber compounds break down, and they need to be replaced.
- During a race, the car's cockpit temperature may reach 130 degrees Fahrenheit or more, and the steel roll cage may be even hotter.

HOW TO PERFORM A FAST 180-DEGREE TURN WITH YOUR CAR

FROM REVERSE

1 Put the car in reverse.

2 Select a spot straight ahead. Keep your eyes on it, and begin backing up.

3 Jam on the gas.

4 Cut the wheel sharply 90 degrees around (a quarter turn) as you simultaneously drop the transmission into drive.

Make sure you have enough speed to use the momentum of the car to swing it around, but remember that going too fast (greater than 45 mph) can be dangerous and may flip the car (and strip your gears). Turning the wheel left will swing the rear of the car left; turning it right will swing the car right.

5 When the car has completed the turn, step on the gas and head off.

From reverse*

While backing up, jam on the gas. Cut the wheel a quarter turn, and simultaneously drop into drive.

Vehicle pivots at the rear wheel.

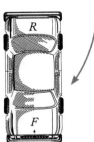

The momentum of the car effectuates the turn.

*At speeds no greater than 45 mph

From Drive

1 While in drive, or a forward gear, accelerate to a moderate rate of speed (anything faster than 45 mph risks flipping the car).

2 Slip the car into neutral to prevent the front wheels from spinning.

3 Take your foot off the gas and turn the wheel 90 degrees (a quarter turn) while pulling hard on the emergency brake.

4 As the rear swings around, return the wheel to its original position and put the car back into drive.

5 Step on the gas to start moving in the direction from which you came.

Be Aware

- The 180-degree turn while moving forward is more difficult for the following reasons:
- It is easier to swing the front of the car around, because it is heavier and it will move faster with momentum.
- It is harder to maintain control of the rear of the car—it is lighter and will slip more easily than the front. Spinning out of control, or flipping the car, are potential dangers.
- Road conditions can play a significant role in the success—and safety—of this maneuver. Any surface without sufficient traction (dirt, mud, ice, gravel) will make quick turns harder and collisions more likely.

how to perform a past 180-degree turn with your car

HOW TO SURVIVE
A MOTORCYCLE
SPINOUT

1 | **Remain on the bike.**
Try to regain control until the last possible moment. Even if you feel the bike begin to slide, the tires may regain traction in an instant, allowing you to recover and ride away. If the spinout is unavoidable, execute a low-side crash, wherein the bike slides out and away from you as you slide in the same direction, but behind the bike.

2 | **Apply both brakes.**
As you feel the wheels lose traction, squeeze the brake lever with your right hand to apply the front brake, and press down on the pedal with your right foot to apply the rear brake. With both brakes locked, the bike will keep sliding out, eliminating the possibility of the wheels regaining traction and throwing you over the high side.

3 | **Slide.**
Stay on your back as you slide, with your helmet slightly raised so you can see any approaching obstructions. Keep arms and legs slightly spread to distribute your body weight evenly and to reduce the possibility of a head-over-heels tumble.

4 Once you have come to a stop, stay still.

Do not try to stand up until your slide has stopped completely. You will pitch forward if you try to get up before your slide has completely stopped.

5 Get up slowly.

Check for injuries. If you were wearing full leathers, pads, gloves, and a helmet, you should be relatively uninjured.

6 Check the bike.

There is little chance of an explosion after a spinout, so it is safe to approach your motorcycle and look for damage.

Be Aware

- A high-side crash, in which the bike begins to slide in one direction, suddenly regains traction, and throws you across it in the opposite direction, is much more dangerous than a low-side crash and slide.

- Very few motorcycles have antilock brakes, so applying full braking is an effective way to lock the wheels and continue a low-side spinout.

- Motorcycles are highly sensitive to steering and brake application, and are not very forgiving. To avoid spinouts, always apply fast, smooth, gentle pressure and avoid jerky movements.

HOW TO BAIL OUT OF A STREET LUGE

1 Stay with your board.

Hold on to your board (even if it is broken), and use it to absorb some of the force of the impact. Do not reach out to grab passing objects or drag your legs to try to slow the luge, or you will risk serious injury. Keep your feet on the pegs and your hands on the handles with your back straight throughout the crash. Your helmet, full leathers, and pads will reduce road rash and also help to limit injury.

2 If you are separated from your luge, slide on your back, with your feet pointing downhill.

Do not roll. Rolling will result in more damage to your knees and elbows.

3 Slow your speed with your hands.

Move your arms to a 45 degree angle to your body. Place your gloved hands, palms down, on the road surface. Use the friction created by your gloves to slow your slide and control its direction. Adding pressure with your right hand will alter your slide path to the right, while pressure on your left hand will move you left. Expect to slide at least 200 feet (or triple that, if the road is wet) or until you hit an obstruction.

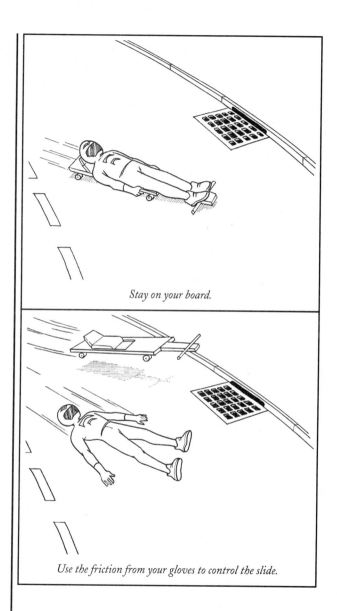

Stay on your board.

Use the friction from your gloves to control the slide.

4 Absorb the impact of the crash.

If an impact is unavoidable, bend your knees slightly to absorb the force of the crash feet first. Keep your toes pointed up, and hit the object with the balls of your feet, not your heels.

Be Aware

- A wheel coming off at speed is the most common street luge equipment failure.
- A truck that is too loose may not be noticeable until you are at speed, when severe wobbling will throw you from the board.
- Race luges do not have brakes.
- Spine, elbow, and knee pads are recommended to reduce serious injury.

How to Survive Being Car-Doored

Throw your weight backward at the moment of impact. Stand up on the pedals and apply the rear brakes only. Turn your body to hit the door with your side to disperse the impact.

HOW TO TREAT
A HOCKEY PUCK
TO THE EYE

1 Place the victim on his back.
Lying with the eye facing up reduces the chance of leakage of the liquid inside the eyeball.

2 Elevate the head slightly.
Place a folded jacket or towel underneath the victim's head, elevating it slightly above the level of the heart to reduce pressure inside the skull and the eyeball.

3 Apply a cold compress.
Place ice in a plastic bag. Do not apply the compress directly to the skin; use a layer of clothing or plastic to prevent tissue from freezing. Hold the compress gently on the tissue surrounding the eye. Avoid pushing or putting pressure on the eye.

4 Offer pain medication.
If the victim is conscious, administer 600 mgs of ibuprofen. If ibuprofen is not available, use acetaminophen. Avoid administering aspirin: it may cause excess bleeding, which can be harmful during an eye operation.

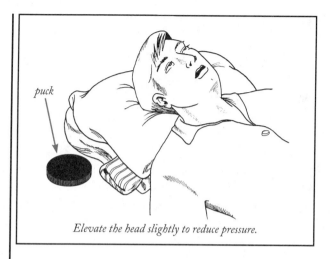

puck

Elevate the head slightly to reduce pressure.

5 Get help.

Tell the emergency operator that you require an emergency room with a qualified ophthalmologist and ear-nose-throat (ENT) surgeon on call.

Be Aware

• A hockey puck to the head may fracture the socket containing the eye and/or rupture the eyeball itself. Both conditions require immediate medical attention.

• Always ask the victim about allergies to medicine before administering any drugs, even ibuprofen.

HOW TO FLIP AN OVERTURNED KAYAK

1 Bend forward at the waist.
Being upside down in a kayak puts your entire torso underwater, making it impossible to breathe. Do not thrash about in the water, which is only likely to empty your lungs of air and make your situation worse. When your kayak overturns, curl at the waist and count to three to help you regain your calm as the kayak naturally aligns in a stable position in the turbulent water. Keep a tight grip on your paddle.

2 Lean toward the left side of the boat.
Flex at the hip to hold yourself in position.

3 Line up your paddle parallel to the kayak.
Hold the paddle firmly in both hands.

4 Sweep the paddle blade away from the boat.
With your right hand, which will be closest to the bow (front) of the kayak, move the paddle outward, keeping it just beneath the surface of the water.

5 Lean upward.
Move your head and torso as close to the surface as possible, resisting the urge to pull your head completely out of the water.

Sweep the paddle away from the boat, moving your head and torso closer to the surface.

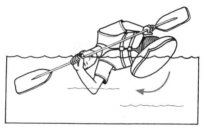

Rotate your hips so you are leaning all the way to the right.

As the kayak rights itself, pull your shoulders and head back into an upright position.

6 Snap your hips to flip the kayak.

As your sweeping paddle motion is midway to completion, quickly snap your hips in one fluid motion so that
instead of leaning your torso all the way toward your
left side, you will be leaning all the way to the right
as the kayak comes underneath your center of gravity.
The friction of your paddle in the water will combine
with the hip snap to create enough momentum to flip
the boat partially onto its keel. Your head and torso
will still be touching the water's surface.

7 Recover your stability.

In a fluid continuation of the flip, bend your torso out
of the water, using your legs and abdominal muscles
to bring the kayak closer to your head. As the kayak
begins to sit upright in the water, whip your head from
the water surface and sit up straight.

Be Aware

• Kayaks flip easily in turbulent water. If you are not
confident in your kayaking skills, or if you lack ex-
perence in fast-moving water, practice flipping the
kayak over in still water until you gain confidence.
• Wear a nose-clip when kayaking in choppy water to
pinch your nostrils together and prevent water from
rushing into your nasal passages.

SURVIVAL TIME IN WATER

Water conducts heat about 25 times more efficiently than air, which is why hypothermia and wetness often go together. Even warm water can lower your body temperature to a dangerous level.

Water Temperature	Loss of Dexterity	Exhaustion/ Unconsciousness	Estimated Survival Time
32.5°F	Less than 2 minutes	Less than 15 minutes	15–45 minutes
32.5–40°F	Less than 3 minutes	15–30 minutes	15–90 minutes
40–50°F	Less than 5 minutes	30–60 minutes	30 minutes– 3 hours
50–60°F	10–15 minutes	1–2 hours	1–6 hours
60–70°F	30–40 minutes	2–7 hours	2–40 hours
70–80°F	1–2 hours	2–12 hours	3 hours+
Over 80°F	2–12 hours	Unlikely	Indefinite

How to Remove a Fishhook
from your Finger

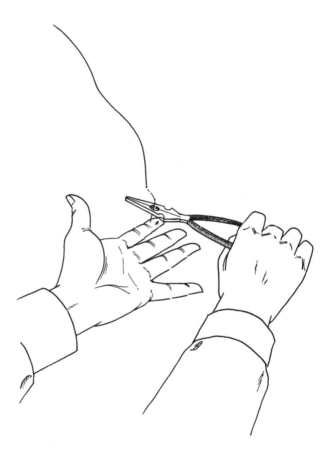

Clip off the end of the hook with a pair of needle-nosed pliers. Pull the unbarbed end of the hook through the wound to remove. Apply antiseptic and dress the injury site.

HOW TO RESCUE A CREW MEMBER OVERBOARD

1 Stop rowing.
As soon as a team member falls off the scull, cease rowing.

2 Coordinate strokes.
Position the boat to within an oar's length of the victim.

Stop rowing.

3 | Perform an extension rescue.
The person closest to the teammate in the water should extend an oar to the victim, making sure not to hit him with it. If the victim is injured or otherwise unable to grab the oar, the rescue must take place in the water; skip to step 7.

4 | Pull the victim close to the boat.

5 | Hold the victim against the side of the boat.
Do not attempt to bring him on board (or let him climb in), or you will risk capsizing the craft.

6 | Row the boat to shore.

7 | Enter the water.
Dive from the boat (or swim from shore) to the downed rower.

8 | Approach the victim from the rear.

9 | Perform a double armpit tow.
Facing the victim from behind, place your dominant arm under one of the victim's arms. Extend your arm across the victim's chest and grab him under the opposite armpit.

10 | Tow the victim to safety.
Using a breaststroke or sidestroke kick, swim the victim back to the boat, to a trailing boat, or to shore.

HOW TO SAIL THROUGH A TYPHOON

1 Reduce speed.

2 Determine your position.
Plot your position on your chart relative to the position of the storm, wind direction and speed, and estimated time to your destination.

3 Adjust your course.
Navigate towards the closest shoreline.

4 Instruct all passengers to put on their personal flotation devices immediately.
Put on your life jacket as well.

5 Assign specific duties to each passenger.
Instruct one crew member to look out for danger areas, debris, or other boats, and another to turn on all bilge pumps.

6 Close hatches, ports, and windows.

7 Secure loose items.
Move loose items below deck. Tie down anything that cannot be moved below deck.

Tie down anything that cannot be moved below deck.

8 Lower the sails or change to storm sails.

9 Prepare the life boat.
Equip with emergency food, water, and first aid kit.

10 Unplug any electrical equipment.
Turn off circuit breakers and disconnect antennas. Instruct passengers and crew to avoid contact with metal objects.

11 Direct the bow into winds.
Approach waves at a 40- to 45-degree angle.

12 Keep passengers low and to the center of the boat.
Rig jack lines, life lines, and safety harnesses to anyone that needs to be on deck.

Be Aware

- Clouds are the best indicators of weather. Watch for stratus clouds that lower or cumulus clouds that rise up and turn into cumulonimbus clouds, both indicators of approaching storms.
- When you first realize you are facing inclement weather, radio into the Coast Guard, as well as other boats. Inform them of your location and float plan.
- There are three main distress calls on the VHF radio:
    MAYDAY: Grave and imminent danger to life or vessel (fire, person overboard, etc.)
    PAN-PAN: Help needed (less severe than Mayday)
    SECURITÉ: Hazards to navigation

HOW TO DISARM
AN IRATE GOLFER

1 Determine the level of danger.
If a golfer is waving a club around angrily or drunkenly, or is exhibiting undue hostility, it may be necessary to act quickly to restore order and safety.

2 Try to talk him down.
Speak calmly, keeping your tone even and your voice low. Do not make sudden gestures or movements. Remind him that it's only a game. Tell him to take a few deep breaths.

3 If he threatens to strike, quickly move into the center of the potential swing.
As he draws the club back to swing at you, approach him at an angle that will bring you to the center of the club. Try to remain close to his body. You are much more likely to be injured by the outer end of the club.

4 Grab the club.
At the top of his swing, or just as the club starts to descend, step close to him and, using one or both hands, clutch the club tightly near the grip. Pull down, staying close to him, until you can wrap your arm around the club. Hold the shaft with your armpit while keeping a firm grasp on the club's grip.

grab here

Grab the club of the irate golfer
as it starts to descend or at the top
of the swing.

Tuck the club under your armpit
and wrench it away by rotating
away from the irate golfer.

5 Wrench the club away.
Maintaining your hold, rotate your body around, away from the golfer's face. This maneuver should give you the leverage you need to wrench the club out of his grip. Pull with just enough force to free the club from his grasp.

6 Step back quickly, and be prepared for him to continue to be angry and to flail.
If necessary, use the club to keep him away from his bag, where he might obtain a second weapon.

7 If necessary, call for help.
Seek the assistance of your fellow golfers to help defuse the situation.

8 Continue to talk to him until he calms down.

Be Aware
It is always advisable to make all possible attempts to avoid physical confrontation. Your first choice should be to ignore and walk away from an irate golfer. Your next choice should be to use verbal skills to calm the golfer by speaking in low tones and showing understanding. Become physical only as a last resort, to avoid greater injury to yourself or others.

HOW TO CONTROL YOUR GOLF RAGE

1 Immediately set down anything you might be inclined to break or use as a weapon.

Drop your clubs, bags, balls, spike-cleaning tools, golf shoes—anything you might use to injure another golfer.

2 Take ten deep breaths.

Breathe by expanding your stomach and abdomen, not your chest. This will cause the oxygen to enter your bloodstream more quickly, calming you down.

3 Repeat the following words to yourself as you breathe: "It's just a game. It's just a game."

Putting the cause of your anger in perspective may help prevent you from causing harm.

4 If you feel you have been wronged, say so.

Be polite but assertive—explain clearly to the person involved why you are angry. Limit the discussion to the specific cause of your anger—do not get into bigger issues such as, "You always act this way."

5 Avoid making inflammatory statements.

Making value-judgment and personal insults or implying illegal tactics will not be helpful.

6 Listen and tolerate.

Inevitably, the object of your anger will have a few thoughts of his own. Let him talk—this will decrease the likelihood of a further argument, and increase the likelihood of a resolution. Try to see the situation through the other person's eyes, even if this is difficult. The person you are speaking with will likely follow suit.

7 Forgive yourself or the other person for the infraction.

8 Laugh it off.

Try to defuse the situation with humor. Laughter, especially when it comes to golf, is often the best medicine.

Be Aware

However tempting it may be, taking your anger out on an inanimate object such as your clubs, your ball, or your golf cart may only lead to you hurting yourself or irreparably damaging the object. To release your anger, squeeze a golf ball or a plush toy you carry for this purpose.

HOW TO PLAY OUT
OF A WATER TRAP

1 Determine what is under your ball.
Ascertain what is beneath the water and whether you
are hitting off sand or a rock bed before you take the
shot. Unknowingly swinging into a hard surface can
do significant damage to your hands or wrists and your
club.

2 Calculate the ball's depth.
The more of the ball that is showing above the water
line, the better. The reliability of executing this shot
decreases considerably if the top of the ball is more
than half an inch below the water line.

3 Take off your shoes and socks.
If you cannot stand on the bank, step into the water
barefoot.

Try to determine what is underneath your ball before you swing.
Unknowingly hitting a hard surface may damage your hands,
wrists, or club.

Open the club face slightly. Aim behind the ball, swing down and through it.

4 | Wear a raincoat or other foul-weather gear.
There will be a large spray that may include mud.

5 | Grip the club firmly.
Because the club will be moving through something with a high resistance—water—the club head will twist if you do not maintain a firm hold.

6 | Open the club head slightly.
The club head will naturally close as the club moves through the water.

7 Aim behind the ball.

Play the shot as if the ball were buried in the sand. Hit the water approximately one ball length behind the ball. Do not be concerned about refraction of the light through the water; the ball is not deep enough for this to be a factor.

8 Swing down and through the ball.

Hit the ball hard. It will be the force of the water behind the ball that carries the ball out, not the impact with the club face itself.

Be Aware

- Going into or near the water may not be a good idea due to the possible presence of snakes, alligators, and other animals, particularly in natural water hazards. Courses along the ocean or deep lakes pose issues of general water safety. Check for posted signs throughout the course that warn of local hazards or dangerous animals.
- Check the back of the scorecard for local rules that might apply to hitting out of the water.
- Your club cannot make contact with the water in the hazard prior to your shot. If contact is made, a two-stroke penalty will be assessed or in match play you will lose the hole.

HOW TO SURVIVE BEING HIT IN THE GOOLIES

"Goolies" is a Scottish term, used at St. Andrews and elsewhere, that refers to the "privates," or the groin area.

1 **Lie down immediately.**
Do not walk around. Cover your private parts to shield the area from further injury (and embarrassment). Clutching yourself will probably be your natural reaction to being hit by a club head or ball.

2 **Apply a cold pack to the injured area to reduce swelling.**
Use ice in a bag or cloth, or a cold can of soda or beer. This will help reduce the swelling and the pain.

3 **Do not apply too much pressure.**
Extreme pressure may cause more pain.

4 **If the pain is significant and does not subside within a few minutes, inspect the injury.**
Remove your pants to get a better look at the swelling and check for any irregularities.

5 **If the pain lasts more than an hour, or if the area is significantly bruised, seek medical attention.**

HOW TO SURVIVE BEING CHASED BY A PACK OF DOGS WHILE JOGGING

Enter a car or nearby building as quickly as possible. Some breeds will tire after a short chase, while others may continue to chase you over long distances. Climb a tree only if you are able to get more than 4 feet off the ground.

HOW TO TREAT A GYM ADDICTION

1 Examine your behavior.
- Do you work out multiple times a day?
- Do you show up at the gym when you know it is not open?
- Do fellow gym-goers think you are an employee of the gym?
- Have you ever lied to family members or friends about the amount of time you spend at the gym?
- Do you have designated equipment that no one else is allowed to use?
- Do you consistently and repeatedly exceed the time limit on the treadmill?
- Does the thought of your gym closing for a holiday terrify you?

2 Admit that you have a problem and that you need help. Realize that you are not responsible for your disease—but you are responsible for your recovery. Make recovery a priority.

3 Admit to one other person that you have a problem. This person will help you wean yourself off the gym. This person should not work at the gym.

Admit that you have a problem.

how to treat a gym addiction

4 Reduce the amount of time you spend at the gym.
Replace your gym time with other activities to take
your mind off the withdrawal you may experience.
Make it a point to engage in activities that do not
involve exercise. Read a magazine, go to the movies,
or take a nap.

5 Watch yourself carefully and be willing to forgive
a relapse.
Be prepared to relapse, which is a common occurrence
on the road to recovery. If you fall back into your old
gym habits, admit it to yourself and seek out others
for support.

6 Do not be afraid to ask for help when you need it.
Consult a therapist. Form or join a support group for
other exercise addicts.

7 Remember that no one is perfect.
Seek the ability to change the things you can, and to
accept the things you cannot change.

Be Aware
Replacing gym habits with workouts at home is a sign
of addiction, not a step to recovery.

How to Stop an Out-of-Control Treadmill

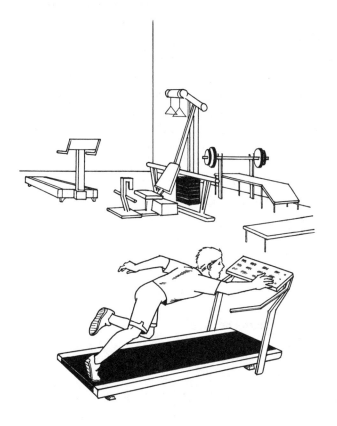

Sprint a step faster and lunge for the "kill switch" or yank the red power "key" from its socket on the control panel. If you cannot reach the control panel, keep pace as best you can and call for help.

HOW TO SPOT A CARD CHEAT

⭐ Examine the cards.

Before play begins, look for irregularities in the cards that might help a cheater identify a particular card. Marks in a round design, like marks on a clock face, may indicate the value of a card; an ace is marked at one o'clock, an eight at eight o'clock. Nicks, nail marks, stains, and crimps may also be marks. Beware if a player bends cards during play.

⭐ Watch for false shuffling.

Confirm that the dealer actually shuffles the deck; a cheat may have brought in a prestacked deck. An overhand shuffle can stack a deck right in front of your eyes. Insist on a reshuffle if you are suspicious. Require that the deck be cut by someone other than the dealer.

⭐ Watch for team cheating.

Shufflers who first bend the deck can be sending a signal to the cutter where to cut the deck; the bent half of the deck should be easy to spot when the deck is placed on the table for the cutter. A cheater can also leave a slight jog in the deck indicating to the accomplice where to make the cut.

watch the
dealer shuffle

*Watch for facial expressions, body language, or other nonverbal
cues that can be used to signal another player.*

★ Listen for verbal cues between partners.

Repeated phrases may have hidden meanings. Be suspicious of players (or nonplayers) who wander the room, then interact with another player. Signals can also include nonverbal cues such as facial expressions, body language, gestures, and subtle indicators such as sighs or sneezes.

★ Watch the banker.

Keep an eye on the tender of the pot, the banker, or other special task holders. Cheaters can palm a chip when distributing winnings, skim off bank winnings, short change a player, or otherwise sweeten their own winnings.

Be Aware

• Mirrors, windows, and even eyeglasses (especially reflective sunglasses) can reflect a player's hand.

• Draw cards to determine who sits where to decrease cooperative cheating.

• Make a rule that someone other than the dealer shuffles the cards.

• The deck should sit squarely on the table. An even slightly spread deck can reveal marks to a cheater.

• Require that players keep cards on the table at all times.

• Do not be fooled by a good hand; a cheat may deal you a good hand, but his will be better.

• Use a position or joker on the bottom of the deck so that no one can see the bottom card and the dealer cannot deal from the bottom of the deck.

How to Play a Blackjack Hand

H: Hit / S: Stay / DD: Double Down

	2	3	4	5	6	7	8	9	10	A
8	H	H	H	H	H	H	H	H	H	H
9	H	DD	DD	DD	DD	H	H	H	H	H
10	DD	DD	DD	DD	DD	DD	DD	DD	H	H
11	DD	DD	DD	DD	DD	DD	DD	DD	DD	H
12	H	H	S	S	S	H	H	H	H	H
13	S	S	S	S	S	H	H	H	H	H
14	S	S	S	S	S	H	H	H	H	H
15	S	S	S	S	S	H	H	H	H	H
16	S	S	S	S	S	H	H	H	H	H
17	S	S	S	S	S	S	S	S	S	S
18	S	S	S	S	S	S	S	S	S	S
19	S	S	S	S	S	S	S	S	S	S
20	S	S	S	S	S	S	S	S	S	S

NOTE: Across the top is what the dealer is showing; what you're holding is down the left side.

POKER TIPS

- **Pick the right time to play.** Never play drunk, or in an extremely good or bad mood.

- **Know when to hold 'em and/or fold 'em.** Only get into hands when you know you've got the goods, and fold frequently. Avoid the classic rookie mistake of throwing good money after bad; once you know you've been beat, fold, no matter what you've already added to the pot.

- **Mix it up.** Very occasionally, violate the previous rule, for example, by knowingly playing a terrible hand, to create the impression of unpredictability.

- **Spot your opponent's tells.** Signs that a player has a good hand include trembling hands, frequent checking of his chip stack, and asking lots of questions, such as "Is it my bet?" and "What's the bet?" Signs of a poor hand include exaggerated smiling, terse conversation, and staring at the flop.

- **Control your tells.** Learn from friends how you give away what kind of hand you have, and train yourself to restrain your body language. Wear oversized hats, sunglasses, and headphones to conceal your reactions.

HOW TO WIN A BAR BET

Make bets that you know you will win, or perform a surefire bar trick for drinks. Select a mark, preferably someone who has been drinking heavily.

BRANDY SNIFTER AND CHERRY

You will need a small brandy snifter, an empty glass, and a stemless maraschino cherry.

1 Place the snifter upside down over the cherry.

2 Wager a free drink that you can get the cherry into the empty glass without touching the cherry or empty glass.
The cherry can touch only the snifter, which must remain upside down. Squashing the cherry onto the rim is prohibited.

3 Use centrifugal force.
When he bets, show him the power of centrifugal force. Hold the base of the snifter and rotate it quickly on the bar top. When the cherry starts spinning inside the glass, lift the snifter off the table. Keep rotating the snifter and hold it over the glass. When you slow your rotation, the cherry will drop into the glass. Collect your free drink.

Rotate snifter.

Lift snifter off the table as the cherry spins.

Drop the cherry into the target glass.

A Race to the Finish

1 | **Identify your mark.**
At the bar, find a small group of men drinking together who seem tipsy, but not so drunk that they will try to kill you when played for fools.

2 | **Make your proposition.**
Sit down next to the group, and casually say "You guys want to see something cool?" State the proposed bet simply and clearly: "Anyone want to bet I can drink three beers before you can drink a single shot?"

3 | **Let them decide who will take the bet.**
Faced with a challenge, a group of men will naturally jockey for supremacy by mocking or goading each other into taking the bet.

4 | **Let the mark determine the stakes.**
Allow the other person to set the stakes, especially if his friends are suggesting he will lose. Offer gentle reassurance such as, "It's totally up to you. Whatever you want to make it." And then whatever he proposes, up the ante by saying, "Oh, okay. Or we could make it a real bet. Whatever you want."

5 | **State the rules.**
Clearly say what the bet is and how it works. "I will drink three beers before you drink a single shot. You give me a one-beer head start, and neither of us can touch the other's glasses.

6 Hear it back.

Have the mark repeat the rules back to you, and make sure that all his friends and anyone else present can hear, so there are plenty of witnesses.

7 Put the money on the bar.

Illustrate your commitment to the wager by suggesting that both you and the mark place your money directly on the bar in front of you. This will also allow you to collect the money more easily once you win.

8 Feign second thoughts.

As the bartender brings the drinks, suddenly look anxious and say things such as, "Oh wait, did I get that right?" Try to back out: "You know what? Forget the whole thing." When the mark presses you, relent and agree to go through with it. He may try to raise the stakes of the wager; if so, reluctantly agree.

9 Win the bet.

After you drink your head start beer, place the empty glass over his shot glass. This way he cannot drink his drink, because he's not allowed to touch your glass, per the rules of the bet. Finish your other two beers.

10 Be gracious.

If the mark seems upset, offer to buy him a beer (with his own money) from the winnings on the bar. You've still come out several beers ahead.

HOW TO TREAT
A DART INJURY

1 If the dart is embedded in the head, neck, chest, or back, leave it in place.

Rinse a small, clean towel in cold water, wring it out, and wrap the towel around the base of the dart to stabilize it and prevent further penetrating or shearing injury. Take the person to the hospital, or call for an ambulance.

2 Remove the dart.

If the dart is embedded in an arm or leg, remove it from the victim using a fast, pulling motion. Put the dart in a safe location where it will not cause further injury. (If the dart bounced or has already fallen off the victim, ask where he was hit.)

3 Place the victim in a sitting position.

4 Examine the wound.

If blood is spurting from the wound, apply a clean cloth to the injury site. If there is bleeding but no spurting, skip to step 8.

5 Apply pressure.

Elevate the affected area above the level of the heart. Hold the cloth firmly in place for 5 minutes.

Locate the dart.

6 | **Remove the cloth and check the wound.**
If blood continues to spurt, apply a new, clean cloth, elevate, and apply pressure for 15 additional minutes. Change the cloth as needed. For persistent oozing, apply pressure for 30 minutes.

7 | **Examine the wound.**
Once the wound has stopped spurting, check the injury site, wiping away any seeping blood.

8 | **Rinse.**
When the bleeding has stopped or slowed, gently rinse the wound under cool tap water.

9 Bandage.
Cover with a large, sterile dressing.

10 Clean the dart.
Rinse the dart under hot tap water, then wipe thoroughly with rubbing (isopropyl) alcohol.

11 Remove the victim from the field of play.

Be Aware
A tetanus booster may be required if the victim has not had one in the previous 10 years.

HOW TO TAKE
A PUNCH

A BLOW TO THE BODY

1 Tighten your stomach muscles.
A body blow to the gut (solar plexus) can damage organs and kill. This sort of punch is one of the best and easiest ways to knock someone out. (Harry Houdini died from an unexpected blow to the abdomen.)

2 Do not suck in your stomach if you expect that a punch is imminent.

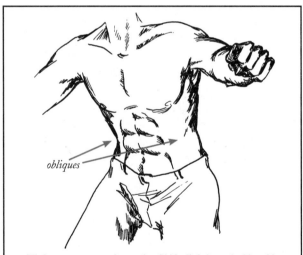

obliques

Tighten your stomach muscles. Shift slightly so the blow hits your side. Absorb the impact with your obliques.

3 If possible, shift slightly so that the blow hits your side, but do not flinch or move away from the punch. Try to absorb the blow with your obliques: this is the set of muscles on your side that wraps around your ribs. While a blow to this area may crack a rib, it is less likely to do damage to internal organs.

A Blow to the Head

1 Move toward the blow, not away from it.
Getting punched while moving backward will result in the head taking the punch at full force. A punch to the face can cause head whipping, where the brain moves suddenly inside the skull, and may result in severe injury or death.

2 Tighten your neck muscles and clench your jaw to avoid scraping of the upper and lower palettes.

deflect the blow with your arm

Tighten your neck and jaw. Clench your teeth. A punch can be absorbed effectively by the forehead.

A Straight Punch

1 The straight punch—one that comes straight at your face—should be countered by moving toward the blow.
This will take force from the blow.

2 A punch can be absorbed most effectively and with the least injury by the forehead.
Avoid taking the punch in the nose, which is extremely painful.

3 Attempt to deflect the blow with an arm.
Moving into the punch may result in your attacker missing the mark wide to either side.

4 (optional) Hit back with an uppercut or roundhouse.

A Roundhouse Punch

1 Clench your jaw.
A punch to the ear causes great pain and can break your jaw.

2 Move in close to your attacker.
Try to make the punch land harmlessly behind your head.

3 (optional) Hit back with an uppercut.

An Uppercut

1 Clench your neck and jaw.
An uppercut can cause much damage, whipping your head back, easily breaking your jaw or your nose.

2 Use your arm to absorb some of the impact or deflect the blow to the side—anything to minimize the impact of a straight punch to the jaw.

3 Do not step into this punch.
If possible, move your head to the side.

4 (optional) Hit back with a straight punch to the face or with an uppercut of your own.

HOW TO WIN A SWORD FIGHT

Always keep your sword in the "ready" position—held in front of you, with both hands, and perpendicular to the ground. With this method, you can move the sword side to side and up and down easily, blocking and landing blows in all directions by moving your arms. Hold the tip of the sword at a bit of an angle, with the tip pointed slightly toward your opponent. Picture a doorway—you should be able to move your sword in any direction and quickly hit any edge of the doorframe.

How to Deflect and Counter a Blow

1 Step up and into the blow, with your arms held against your body.
React quickly and against your instincts, which will tell you to move back and away. By moving closer, you can cut off a blow's power. Avoid extending your arms, which would make your own counterblow less powerful.

2 Push or "punch" at the blow instead of simply trying to absorb it with your own sword.
If a blow is aimed at your head, move your sword completely parallel to the ground and above your head. Block with the center of your sword, not the end. Always move out toward your opponent, even if you are defending and not attacking.

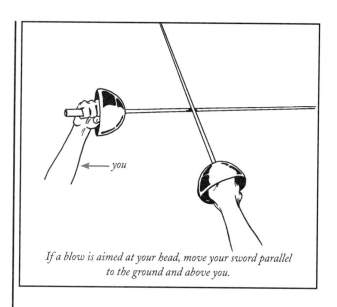

If a blow is aimed at your head, move your sword parallel to the ground and above you.

How to Attack

1 Move the sword in steady, quick blows up and down and to the left and right.

Assuming you must disable your attacker, do not try to stab with your sword. A stabbing motion will put you off balance and will leave your sword far out in front of you, making you vulnerable to a counterblow.

2 Do not raise the sword up behind your head to try a huge blow—you will end up with a sword in your gut.

3 Hold your position, punch out to defend, and strike quickly.

4 | **Wait for your attacker to make a mistake.**
Stepping into a blow or deflecting it to the side will put him/her off balance. Once your opponent is off balance, you can take advantage of their moment of weakness by landing a disabling blow, remembering not to jab with your sword but to strike up and down or from side to side.

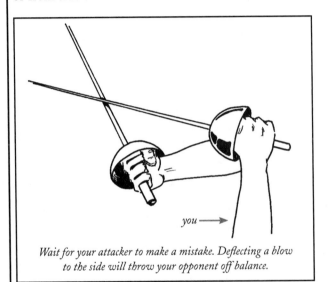

you →

Wait for your attacker to make a mistake. Deflecting a blow to the side will throw your opponent off balance.

How to Deal with a 7/10 Bowling Split

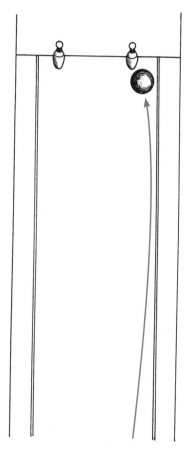

Aim for the far right of the 10 pin if right-handed, the far left of the 7 pin if left-handed. Throw to hit the pin as hard as possible, with significant hook. With luck, the struck pin will bounce off the back wall and knock over the other pin.

TRASH-TALKING INSULTS

You suck!

You stink!

Hit the shower, your game stinks.

I'm gonna beat you like a drum.

Pay attention now, class is in session.

I'm gonna to eat you up and spit out the pieces
    I don't like.

Are you playing the same game I am?

You know the game started, right?

When are you gonna start playing?

When do the real players get here?

Did your mama teach you to play that way?

Did your infant child teach you to play that way?

Not bad—for a six-year-old girl!

Not bad—for a monkey!

Not bad—for a six-year-old girl monkey!

You forget your glasses?

You forget your walker?

You forget how to play?

You need to take a nap?

You need a doctor?

Shuffleboard court is that way.

Tetherball pole is that way.

Ping-pong table is that way.

Have a seat—the grown-ups are playing now.

Bring it!

Bring it on!

How's that feel? That feel good? Bet it don't.
You want me to wake you up when it's over?
Should I call your grandma? She'd probably
    play better.
Stick to losing. You're so good at it.
It's all downhill from here.
When I'm done there will be nothing left of you
    except a shadow.
Say goodnight, the Sandman is here.
I could tell you that you played well, but I'd be lying.
If you'd told me you were so bad, I would have
    spotted you some points.

*Note: When necessary, the word "bitch" may be appended
to any of these.*

HOW TO OPEN A BOTTLE WITHOUT AN OPENER

ANOTHER BOTTLE

1 Hold the bottle you wish to open upright in your nondominant hand.

Grip the neck of the target bottle, placing your index finger over the back edge of the cap.

2 Hold the second bottle horizontally around the label.

Grip this bottle, the opener, as though shaking hands with the bottle.

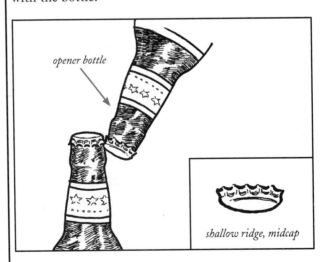

opener bottle

shallow ridge, midcap

3 Fit the shallow ridge found at midcap of the opener bottle under the bottom edge of the cap of the bottle you wish to open.

By using this ridge, and not the bottom of the cap, you will not risk opening the second bottle in step 4.

4 Using the opener bottle as a lever, press down and pry the cap off the target beer bottle.

5 Enjoy.

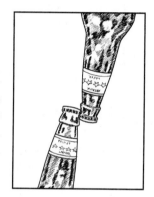

ALTERNATE METHOD
Hold both bottles end to end perpendicular to the ground, with the crimped edges of the caps together, locking them in place. Pull. Be careful, however, as either or both bottle caps could come off.

LIGHTER

1 Grip the bottle in your nondominant hand.
Make a fist around the top of the bottle so that your thumb overlaps your index finger and the web between your thumb and index finger sits in the groove under the cap.

2 Fit the bottom of the lighter under the teeth of the cap.
Position the lighter so that it rests on the middle knuckle of your index finger.

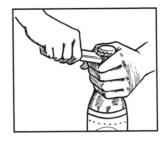

3 Press the top of the lighter down and toward the bottle.
Use the index finger on your dominant hand to provide resistance.

4 Pry off the cap.
If necessary, turn the bottle and repeat.

TABLE EDGE

1 Put the teeth of the bottle cap against the edge of a table.
The cap should be on top of the table edge; the bottle should be below the table. Do not attempt on a soft wood or antique table.

2 Use your fist to hit the bottle.
The bottle will take a downward trajectory, and the cap will pop off.

SCREWDRIVER, SPOON, FORK, OR KNIFE

1 Place the implement under the bottle cap, as high as it will go.

2 Pry off the cap.
Slowly go around the cap and lift up each crimped area with the tool, similar to opening a can of paint.

3 When the cap starts to move, fit the tool higher up under the cap and remove it.

BELT BUCKLE

1 Unfasten your belt buckle. If your pants are in danger of falling down, sit.

2 Pull the "tooth" of the buckle to one side.

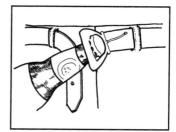

3 Fit the cap into the buckle so that one edge is wedged against the buckle.

4 Pry off.
Pull the bottle slowly. A quick tug may result in a spill.

5 Refasten your belt.

Deadbolt Lock

1 Fit your bottle into the lock. Place the head of the bottle into the recession in a doorframe into which a deadbolt slips, so that the cap fits against the notch in the lock's frame.

2 Pull up slowly. The bottle cap should pop right off.

Fire Hydrant

1 Look for an arrow on top of the hydrant labeled "open."

2 At the end of the arrow, locate the recess between the screw and the nut.

3 Insert the cap into the recess.

4 Press down slowly on the bottle until the cap comes off.

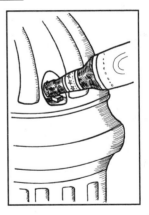

In-Line Skate

1 Place the cap between the shoe and the blade. Hold onto the bottle with your dominant hand. If you are wearing the skate, use the hand opposite the skate to open the bottle.

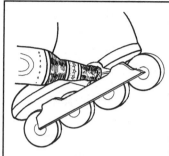

2 Pull up slowly on the bottle and pry off.
Quickly right the bottle to avoid spilling.

Metal Pool Bridge

1 Hold the stick of the bridge in one hand and a beer bottle in the other.
Do not attempt to open over the pool table.

2 Position the cap inside the opening of the bridge.
Fit the cap snugly against the edge.

3 Press down on the bottle. Slowly increase the pressure until the cap loosens. Right the bottle immediately to prevent spillage.

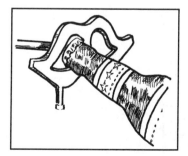

Vending Machine

1 Locate a newspaper, snack, or soda vending machine.
An older soda machine might actually have a bottle opener.

2 Place the cap in the coin return.
Wedge the cap against the top of the opening.

3 Press down slowly until the cap is removed.

Be Aware
Never drink from a bottle with broken or chipped glass.

HOW TO SOBER UP FAST

1 | Avoid pills.
Do not take ibuprofen, acetaminophen, or aspirin just before, during, or after drinking. Acetaminophen may cause liver damage in conjunction with alcohol. Ibuprofen can cause severe stomach irritation. Aspirin thins the blood, which may exacerbate a hangover.

2 | Drink lots of fluids.
Dehydration from alcohol can be treated with water, sweet juices, or sports drinks. Orange juice and tomato juice contain potassium, which will help overcome the shaky feeling of a major hangover.

3 | Take vitamins.
A good multivitamin or vitamin B complex combats vitamin depletion.

4 | Eat.
Starchy foods—bread, crackers, rice, or pasta—break down into sugar, which speeds absorption of alcohol into your system. A spoonful of honey (which is high in fructose) helps to quickly burn off any remaining alcohol in the stomach. Listen to your body's cravings: If eggs sound good, eat them. If something spicy sounds better, eat that. There are no right or wrong things to eat; just take your food slowly and in small amounts.

5 | Rest or sleep for as long as possible.

6 | Repeat steps 2 through 5 if you wake up with a hangover.

How to Prevent a Hangover

- Eat before you begin to drink and snack while drinking.
- If you do not eat, coat your stomach with a full glass of milk.
- Pace yourself and drink water between drinks.
- Drink clear liquors. Some spirits are higher in congeners (impurities) than others: red wine, brandies (including cognac), and whiskies usually have more congeners than other types of alcohol. Generally, the clearer your spirit, the fewer impurities and the less severe the hangover.
- Champagne and mixed drinks made with carbonated sodas allow for faster alcohol absorption; they should be sipped slowly.
- Know your limits. In most states, a Blood Alcohol Content (BAC) of .10 means you are legally drunk— and some states now use the stricter .08 BAC. For most average-size adults, this can mean as few as two drinks in an hour.
- Do not mix your liquors. Each spirit has different toxins that must be processed by your liver. It is best not to overload it.
- Before going to bed, have a snack of a banana or cheese and crackers.

- Keep water beside your bed and drink it if you
  awaken during the night.

How to Deal with "The Spins"

1 Focus your gaze on a stationary object in the room.
Keep your eyes open. Avoid looking at ceiling fans. Stare
at the object for one minute.

2 Close your eyes.

3 Picture the object you were looking at.
Imagine that the object is imprinted on the inside of
your eyelids.

4 Open your eyes.
If the spinning returns, stare at your object for one
minute.

5 Close your eyes.
Repeat steps 3 and 4.

6 Repeat steps 3, 4, and 5 until the spinning stops or
you pass out.

Be Aware
- The spins usually occur when your eyes are closed.
  Watch television, go out for some air, or eat a
  meal—anything to stay awake and keep your eyes
  open until you sober up.

- Eating reduces drinking-related sickness by reducing the speed at which alcohol in the stomach is absorbed into the bloodstream. Eat before drinking: Once you have the spins, it is too late.
- Alcohol is a diuretic and dehydrates. After drinking, replace lost fluid, vitamins, and electrolytes by consuming sports drinks. Avoid drinking excessive amounts of plain water, which will dilute the sodium concentration in the body.

HOW TO VOMIT CORRECTLY

1 Be prepared.
Vomiting may be preceded by sweating, nausea, gagging, increased saliva, or the sensation of swelling under the tongue.

2 Move quickly.
Get to a quiet bathroom or a private area with an appropriate receptacle, such as a toilet, trash can, or metal bowl. If outdoors, look for an area secluded by trees or bushes. Avoid public spaces.

3 Remove necktie or necklace.

4 Open collar.
Unbutton your shirt at least two buttons and pull the sides apart. If you are wearing a pullover, remove it completely, if time permits. Tie back long hair.

5 Relax.
Do not resist.

6 Target a destination.
Vomit into the receptacle. If vomiting into a toilet, grip the sides for support.

7 Wait.
The first bout of vomiting may not be the last. Wait several minutes to make sure you remain in control.

8 Clean up.
Wash your hands and face, rinse out your mouth, and brush your teeth.

9 Return to the party.

HOW TO SURVIVE A STADIUM RIOT

1 Scan the crowd.
Quickly determine the focus of the rioting: mascot, goalpost, star player, referee, fans, band members, coaches, or cheerleaders. Physically distance yourself as quickly as possible.

2 Hide any obvious school affiliation.
If the mob appears to be attacking your school's fans, remove any clothing items with school colors, letters, or emblems. Stuff these items into a nondescript bookbag or plastic bag. Wrap your arms around your bag and use it to shield your torso as you begin your escape. If you do not have an appropriate carryall, leave your school gear behind.

3 Create a protective helmet.
Stuff crumpled-up newspaper or cardboard inside your hat for cushioning. If you do not have a hat, place an empty popcorn tub or other container over your head.

4 Move away from the mascots.
Regardless of whether they are the focus of the riot, both teams' mascots are especially vulnerable to attack. Stay well clear of either mascot.

Move quickly away from the mascots.

5 Observe movement patterns.
Most rioters move en masse in a single direction toward a particular object. Determine which way the mob is headed.

6 Watch for projectiles.
Bend your knees and keep your head low to avoid flying cans, bottles, pennants, water balloons, rocks, pipes, benches, people, or other objects.

7 Move sideways through the crowd to the nearest exit.
Avoid moving forward (toward the center of the riot) or backward (against the surging mob).

Be Aware
If you're the cause of the riot due to your actions as a fan, player, or mascot, ditch your uniform or suit and run.

HOW TO SURVIVE A HOT DOG EATING CONTEST

1 Stand close to the table.

2 Lean slightly forward.

3 Remove the first hot dog from the bun.
Place the bun within immediate reach on the table.

4 Tear the hot dog in half.

5 Shove the two pieces of hot dog, side by side, into your mouth.

6 Chew and swallow.
While chewing and swallowing, pick up the bun and dunk it in your cup of water.

7 Eat the bun.
Insert the entire water-logged bun in your mouth; rapidly chew and swallow it while picking up the next hot dog and breaking it in half.

8 Repeat steps 3 through 7 until time is called.

Dunk the hot dog bun in water to ease swallowing.

9 Drink water after every third hot dog.

Drink enough to lubricate your esophagus, allowing the hot dogs to go down smoothly. Do not drink too much, or your stomach will fill up with water.

10 Swallow and open.

At the end of the competition, swallow whatever is in your mouth and open to show that it is empty.

⭐ **Expand your stomach.**
In the weeks before the competition, drink lots of water and eat nonfattening foods like celery, pineapple, and cabbage.

⭐ **Do not fast.**
Extreme hunger will shrink your stomach and make you a poorer competitor.

⭐ **Eat a light breakfast.**
On the morning of the competition, eat slightly less than usual. Arrive at the contest hungry but not excessively so.

Be Aware
• Partially eaten hot dogs count towards the total number eaten, and are judged in increments of one-eighth of a hot dog.
• Water refills are provided throughout the competition.
• "Reversal" (vomiting) is an immediate disqualifier.

CHAPTER 3
LOVE AND SEX

HOW TO FEND OFF COMPETITORS FOR YOUR DATE

1 Evaluate the situation.
Are you on a first date that is not going well? Is your date paying more attention to the interloper than to you? Do you want to continue dating this person?

2 Determine the seriousness of the offense.
Is it a passing rude drunk, a persistent boor, or someone seriously interested in leaving with your date? How big is the interloper? These factors will determine your response.

3 Stand your ground.
Put your arms around your date, whisper in her ear, and kiss and caress her. Show the suitor that your date is enamored with you, and you with her.

4 Place yourself in the "pickup screen" position.
Wedge yourself between the suitor and your date, with your back to the suitor. Try to block the suitor's path of vision. An "accidental" bump or push with your shoulders or buttocks may be appropriate.

Assume the "pickup screen" position by wedging yourself between the suitor and your date, with your back to the suitor. Try to block the suitor's path of vision.

5 Ask the interloper to stop.
Politely but firmly explain that you are trying to have a conversation with your date and that you would both prefer to be left alone. If the suitor persists, use humor or sarcasm to diffuse the situation. Tell him you can offer him a few phone numbers, or tell him that tonight she's taken, but you will let him know when she's available.

6 If the suitor is with friends, enlist their help to rein him in.

7 Ask your date to tell the suitor to back off.
Your date should tell him that she's flattered but not interested.

8 Try to leave.
If given the choice, choose flight over fight. Suggest to your date that you both move to a table or go to a new establishment. A fight generally doesn't make the evening go any better.

How to Treat a Black Eye

1 Make a cold compress.
Put crushed ice in a plastic bag and wrap the bag in a thin piece of cloth. Alternatively, use a bag of frozen vegetables or a cold, raw steak.

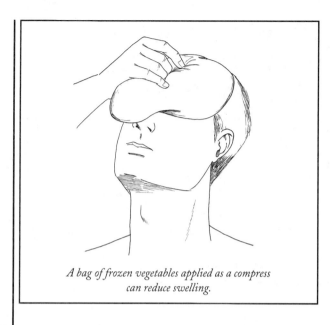

A bag of frozen vegetables applied as a compress can reduce swelling.

2 Sit down, tilt your head back, and cover your eye with the compress.

Use minimal pressure. This position allows gravity to aid in swelling reduction. If the compress is too cold to hold over your eye, use a thicker cloth. Keep the compress over your eye for an hour.

3 Take a painkiller.

For pain, take acetaminophen or ibuprofen.

HOW TO GET
AN EMERGENCY
RESERVATION

BRIBE

1 Determine how much to offer the maitre d' as a bribe. The right amount will depend on the exclusivity and reputation of the establishment. Offer a minimum of $20. You usually get only one chance to try the bribe.

2 Fold the bill into your right palm.
Hold it between your thumb and forefinger.

3 Pass the bribe.
Shake his hand as you tell him how you are sure that he understands how important this night is to you. Be prepared, however, for the occasional maitre d' who takes your money and does not honor your request.

SOB STORY

1 Talk calmly to the maitre d'.
Controlled pleading can prove effective if you bend the right ear at the right time. A friendly, familiar demeanor is most likely to get the first available table. A whiny or arrogant voice will not help at all. If the maitre d' looks harried, wait until he or she has a moment to focus on you.

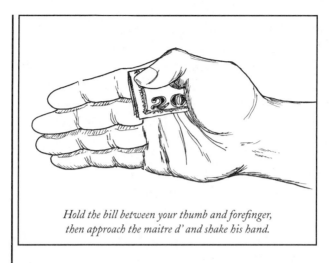

Hold the bill between your thumb and forefinger,
then approach the maitre d' and shake his hand.

2 | Explain your situation.
Be sure to stress the importance of the evening and the special need for a table, embellishing the facts as necessary: an anniversary dinner, a plan to propose marriage (but be prepared to produce a ring), a recovery from a long illness, an overdue reunion.

3 | Speak with emotion.
Catch your voice, have difficulty breathing, shed a tear. You become harder to ignore. Also, the maitre d' will not want you upsetting the other waiting guests and creating a scene.

4 | Appeal to the host's understanding nature.
Create the impression that you would be especially embarrassed in front of your date, since you told her you had a reservation.

| *how to get an emergency reservation*

5 | Look to fellow diners for sympathy.

If you cannot sway the host or maitre d', approach other diners and bribe or persuade them into giving up their table. Use the special event strategy (step 2, above). However, be careful to avoid offending the patrons or embarrassing your date. It is best to try this when your date leaves your side for a moment.

6 | Pull rank.

Your final option is to play the "do you know who I am?" card. Unfortunately, you actually have to be somebody for this one to work.

Be Aware

- Do not try the "lost reservation" ploy; no one believes it anyway. Claiming that the restaurant is at fault for misplacing your reservation provokes confrontation rather than conciliation, and rarely results in a table.
- You can try the "celebrity name drop," but it could backfire. Asking for a table in the name of a celebrity will sometimes get you seated even though the celebrity is "late" in arriving, but the host may also ask you to wait until your group is all present before seating you—and you will be precluded from using other tactics.

HOW TO SURVIVE
IF YOU HAVE
EXCESSIVE GAS

1 Limit your lactose intake during the date.
Many people suffer from an inability to digest milk sugar, or lactose. Colon bacteria ferment the milk sugar, forming a gas that creates a bloated feeling. Keep your intake to less than half a cup at a sitting, and avoid dairy products before your date.

2 Eat a small meal.
Eating a huge dinner on a date is a sure-fire way to precipitate gas.

3 Avoid gas-forming foods.
Bacteria ferment the indigestible carbohydrates in beans, broccoli, cabbage, and other vegetables and fruits into gases.

4 Drink peppermint tea.
Replace an after-dinner drink with a cup or two of peppermint tea. This herb may give you some relief from the gas discomfort that follows a meal.

5 Emit the gas in private.
As a last resort, head to the bathroom. If you feel bloated but are unable to pass gas easily, you can facilitate the emission of gas as follows:

Kneel on the floor, bend forward, and stretch your arms out in front of you. Keep your buttocks high in the air, forming a triangle with your upper body and the floor.

Place paper towels on the floor. Kneel on the towels, bend forward to the floor, and stretch your arms out in front of you. Keep your buttocks high in the air, forming a triangle with your upper body and the floor. This position will force out the unwanted gas and relieve the pressure.

Be Aware

- On average, humans produce ¾ of a liter of gas daily, which is released 11 to 14 times a day.
- Men typically produce more gas than women because they consume more food.

GASSY FOODS TO AVOID

No two digestive systems are alike. Experiment with foods to determine which ones affect you most. In the meantime, exercise caution around the following high-risk items:

- Beans (particularly baked beans)
- Borscht
- Broccoli
- Brussels sprouts
- Cabbage
- Carbonated beverages
- Cauliflower
- Chili
- Cucumbers
- Fatty foods
- Fresh fruit
- Grains and fiber, especially pumpernickel bread
- Gum
- Onions
- Oysters
- Salads (green)

how to survive if you have excessive gas

HOW TO DEAL WITH BAD BREATH

1 Chew gum or mints.
Excuse yourself from the table and head for the host's desk, where there may be a dish of mints. A waiter or busboy may also be able to give you a piece of gum. Go to the restroom and chew the gum for two minutes, then spit it out. This will get your saliva flowing and keep bad breath at bay for an hour or more. Chewing for more than a few minutes is not necessary. Sugar-free gum is best.

2 Chew parsley, mint, or a cinnamon stick.
On the way to the bathroom, pull your waiter aside and ask for one of these common garnishes. Parsley and fresh mint leaves are natural breath fresheners. A cinnamon stick, if chewed, will also clean your breath; do not use ground or powdered cinnamon. Most bartenders will have a stick on hand.

3 Order a salad or some fresh carrots.
If you cannot leave the table, order coarse foods that can help clean the tongue, a major source of bad breath.

Be Aware
Food odors are generally not as bad as you think, but when possible, avoid onions and garlic during your date.

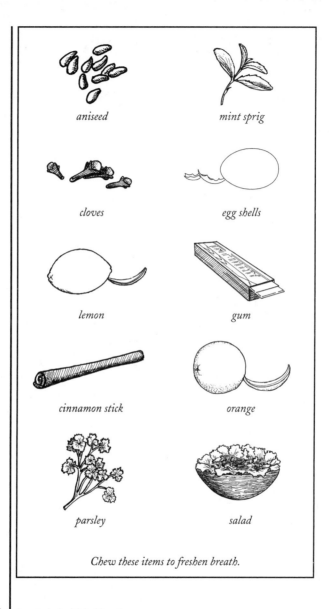

aniseed

mint sprig

cloves

egg shells

lemon

gum

cinnamon stick

orange

parsley

salad

Chew these items to freshen breath.

how to deal with bad breath

1 | Floss.
Before going to bed, floss your teeth. Use unscented floss and smell it after each pass through. Areas that smell the worst need the most attention. Flossing may also help you live longer, as gum disease can shorten your life.

2 | Sweep the tongue.
Gently sweep the mucus off the very back of your tongue with a commercially available tongue cleaner. Avoid cleaners made from sharp metal and do not scrape the tongue.

3 | Brush with mouthwash.
Use an effective mouthwash. Shake if necessary, then pour some into the cap. Dip your toothbrush into it and brush your teeth properly for a few minutes. Do not use mouthwash and toothpaste at the same time as they can cancel out each other's active ingredients. Rinse and gargle with the rest of the mouthwash in the cap.

HOW TO GET INTO AN EXCLUSIVE NIGHTCLUB

1 Wear expensive shoes.
Do not dress sloppily or outlandishly in an attempt to be "unique" or "interesting."

2 Go on a slow night.
Pick a night when fewer people will be trying to get in. Thursday, Friday, and Saturday nights will generally be the most crowded, however Friday and Saturday nights over a holiday weekend can be less crowded as many people head out of town.

3 Travel in a group.
Approach with no more than six people, including at least three women. The women should give no indications of being "taken," such as holding hands with the men in the group; holding hands with one another is okay.

4 Remain calm.
Maintain a laid-back, sober attitude while in line. Do not be argumentative with the doorman, the club staff, or with passersby. Do not name-drop or otherwise try to bluff the doorman into thinking you are more important or interesting than you are. Do not attempt to bribe the doorman or bouncer for entry. Do not

Do not give anyone a "high five."

complain when others arrive and get in while you are waiting. Do not bring a book to read while in line.

5 | Be casual when you do get in.
Nod calmly at the doorman as he waves you inside. Do not give anyone a "high five." Do not begin dancing until you are on the dance floor.

Be Aware

To increase your odds of being allowed in on a subsequent visit:

• Order full bottles rather than individual drinks.
  If there is a price for table service, or for use of a "VIP" area, pay it willingly. Tip at least 35 percent on each round of drinks and food; if possible, calculate the tip without reference to a calculator or wallet-sized tip card.

• If you see celebrities, do not ask for autographs or take photographs. Be polite but not overly flirtatious with the bar staff and cocktail waitresses

• Tip the doorman at least $50 as you exit the club.

HOW TO IDENTIFY
BREAST IMPLANTS

1 Remember: if they look too good to be true, they probably are.

If a woman is over thirty and her breasts defy gravity without a bra or she has a strikingly full and firm upper cleavage and bosom, chances are her breasts are not fully natural. You should also be suspicious of breasts that sit very high on a woman's chest; this is another good sign of implants.

2 Assess breast size as compared to frame size.

Most, though not all, petite women have naturally small breasts.

3 Be suspicious of baseball-shaped breasts or strangely arranged breasts.

In cases of a poor augmentation, the outline of the implant may be noticeable, or the breast may have a very firm, round, baseball-like appearance. Poorly placed implants can often be seen through tight tops. While a good augmentation procedure can be difficult to detect by visual inspection alone, a bad one is quite noticeable.

4 Check cleavage for rippling of the skin.

Implants may ripple in the cleavage or on top of the breasts; look for a wave pattern across the surface.

If a woman is over thirty and has strikingly full breasts that sit very high on her chest, you have reason to be suspicious.

Natural breasts, even very large breasts, although soft, will never have a rippled appearance.

5 If appropriate, brush up against or hug someone with suspected breast implants.
If her breasts feel firmer than normal, implants may be in use.

6 Check under and around the breast for scarring.
In an intimate situation, the opportunity may arise for a closer visual and tactile inspection. Look for scarring under the breasts, around the nipple, and in the armpit area.

HOW TO DATE THREE PEOPLE AT ONCE

⭐ Assign them the same nickname.
Call them all "honey" or "sweetie" or "pumpkin" so that you do not accidentally use the wrong name with the wrong person. It also helps if you discuss the same topics and pick the same song as "our song."

⭐ Keep to a schedule.
See them only on their assigned day—Mary every Thursday, Emily every Friday, and Jenny every Saturday. They will see you as highly disciplined and will not expect to monopolize your time.

⭐ Select three different favorite bars, activities, or restaurants.
A special place for each reduces your chances of running into another date. Look for dimly lit, off-campus locations.

⭐ Be vague.
Provide few details to each date about your whereabouts during nondate evenings. Offer ambiguous responses like "I wish I had time to see you more often, too."

⭐ Keep your answering machine volume turned down.
If you are home with one of your dates and another calls, you will not be found out.

★ **Advise your roommate to say as little as possible.**
Explain your situation and ask for cooperation. Tell your roommate to say only "Nice to see you" when he sees one of your dates. He should avoid "Nice to meet you" or "Nice to see you again" since he may be easily confused about who he is talking to.

★ **Do not place photographs around your room.**
The fewer things and people to explain, the better. Also remove stuffed animals, flowers, cards, mix CDs, or anything that might look like a romantic gift.

★ **Tell everyone that you have a large family.**
Prepare for the time that you will be spotted with another date. If asked later who you were with, you can say she was your cousin.

★ **Refer to several part-time jobs.**
Say that you are sorry to be so unavailable because you are always working. Mention that you are saving all the money you are earning for tuition and other living expenditures so that you don't build expectations about gifts or expensive dates.

★ **Do not boast.**
Aside from your roommate, keep any mention of the simultaneous relationships to yourself. The more people you tell about your multiple assignations, the more likely it is that you will be discovered.

HOW TO REMOVE DIFFICULT CLOTHING

BACK-CLASPING BRA (WITH ONE HAND)

1 Move your date forward.
If your date is lying on her back or leaning against a sofa, you will not have the necessary space to attempt this maneuver. Use a gentle embrace to guide her into a position so that you have access to her back.

2 Visualize the clasp.
Most bras have a hook-and-eye closure. The hooks are generally on her right side; the eyes will be on her left side.

3 Reach your right hand around to the clasp.
Bend your index finger over the bra clasp and place it between the fabric and her skin.

4 Brace your thumb against the eyes of the clasp.

5 Holding your index finger down, push the hook-side of the bra with your thumb.
It may take a few attempts before you get good at this, so do not be discouraged—try again.

6 Slide the now-open bra off her arms.

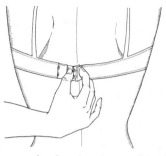

Brace your thumb against the eyes of the clasp.

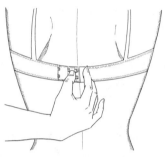

Holding your index finger down, push the hookside of the bra with your thumb.

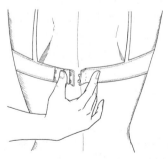

Slide the now-open bra off her arms.

Be Aware
The bigger the breasts, the bigger the challenge, since the closure on her bra is bearing more weight and is likely to be more taut.

Front-Clasping Bra

1 Determine the type of clasp.
There are two different varieties: a pin-in-slot clasp, which has a pin inserted vertically in a slot, and a clicker clasp. Clicker clasps, when closed, often look like a circle or an oval.

2 For a pin-in-slot clasp, pull the pin upward.
This will free the two cups, and you can proceed to step 4.

3 For a clicker clasp, push both ends away from you.
Place your thumbs at the center of the clasp and, using a motion similar to snapping a small wafer in half, apply pressure until it unclicks. Then lift up and separate the two halves of the closure. Depending on the clasp, you will need to raise either the left side or the right side first; try it one way, then the other.

4 Slide the now-open bra off her arms.

Be Aware
To maximize intimacy, maintain eye contact throughout the entire process. Do not look away unless you need to take a quick glance at the closure.

TIGHT BOOTS

1 Sprinkle powder down the shaft of each boot.
Talcum powder or baking powder will reduce the sweat and humidity inside the boots, making them easier to remove.

2 Position your date on the edge of a bed or couch.

3 Position yourself opposite your date.
Sit in a chair braced against a wall, or rest one knee on the floor with the other foot flat on the floor.

4 Cup the heel of the boot in your right hand.
Place your left hand on the area of the boot that covers the front of the leg/shin. Instruct your date to relax the foot in the boot.

5 Pull firmly and steadily with your right hand.
You should feel some give in the heel. When you cannot move the boot anymore, gently rock the boot back and forth. Your date should point the foot only slightly. To avoid injuring the wearer, do not jerk the boot.

6 Slide the boot off slowly.
Caress the newly released foot.

HOW TO HAVE SEX
IN A SMALL SPACE

AIRPLANE LAVATORY

1 **Pick a rendezvous time.**
Select a time when you are least likely to have to wait in line and when you will not be disturbed. The best times are just before the plane reaches cruising altitude or during the in-flight entertainment.

2 **As the plane is ascending, listen for a beep from the in-flight messaging system.**
The first beep comes without a subsequent announcement and indicates to the flight attendants that cruising altitude has almost been reached and that it is safe to begin their preparations. The Fasten Your Seatbelt sign will still be illuminated, but the flight attendants will get up. As soon as the flight attendants clear the aisle, head for the lavatory. Try to select one that is not visible from the galleys. Have your date wait at least a minute, then meet you in the lavatory. You should hear the beverage carts roll by. After a few minutes, the flight attendants will begin to serve drinks, blocking the aisle from passenger access. Alternatively, or in addition, proceed to step 3.

3 **Meet during the movie.**
Plan your rendezvous for the beginning of the film, preferably when the film is at least 15 minutes underway.

Most passengers and flight attendants stay out of the aisles and galley areas during the entertainment portion of the flight, so you will have more privacy. You should proceed to the lavatory first, to be followed a minute later by your date.

4 Put down the toilet seat lid and clean it.
Wipe the seat with sani-wipes if they are available, or use a wet paper towel with soap. Place paper towels or a sanitary toilet seat cover on top for extra protection.

5 Be quiet and be quick.
You will not have a lot of time before people are lining up to get into the restroom.

6 Be ready for turbulence.
The safest positions involve one partner sitting on the closed toilet seat. Then, in the event of bumpy air, neither partner will be too close to the ceiling, risking a concussion.

7 If you do encounter turbulence, hold on.
Brace yourself against the sink and do not try to stand up or move. Stay where you are and ride it out.

8 Exit the lavatory together, feigning illness.
It is illegal to have sex in an airplane bathroom—so deny it in the unlikely event that you are asked. Tell the flight attendant or other passengers that one of you was ill and the other was offering assistance.

Elevator

1 | **Find a building with an older elevator.**
Many older elevators have an emergency stop button that will allow you to halt the elevator. On other units, flipping the switch from run to stop will cause an alarm bell to sound. You will still have plenty of time, at least 10 or 15 minutes, possibly as long as an hour, before firefighters or other emergency personnel are able to access the elevator cabin.

2 | **Alternatively, look for a freight elevator with padding on the walls.**
Freight elevators will be less likely to have an alarm that sounds when the stop switch is thrown. The padding may also muffle sound and provide comfort.

3 | **Look for a camera.**
Virtually all new elevators have security cameras, as do some older ones, including freight elevators. If a camera is present, cover the camera lens—it will probably be in a rear corner—with a piece of tape or with several postage stamps. The security system may include audio as well, however.

4 | **Stop the elevator between floors.**
Elevator doors house a mechanical clutch that opens the corridor (outer) doors. If the elevator is not level with a floor, the corridor doors cannot open, and someone from the outside will not easily be able to open the inner doors.

5 Release the stop button or flip the switch to run when you are ready to leave.

Exit the elevator normally. If emergency personnel are present, tell them there was a malfunction but that you are okay.

Be Aware

If the elevator is stopped level with a floor, an elevator technician will be able to open both the outer (corridor) doors and the inner (elevator) doors from the outside.

Dressing Room

1 Look for a dressing room that has a door and walls that extend to the floor.

If all the dressing rooms have a gap between the floor and the walls, look for one with a secure door, rather than a curtain. If you are in a store that has several dressing rooms, look for the least-trafficked or least-monitored areas. Some dressing rooms have very hard-to-detect security systems—including two-way mirrors—so you cannot guarantee that you will not be seen.

2 Carry clothes as if you are going to try them on.

Trail after a demanding customer who is requiring the attentions of the sales associate on duty. When the employee is occupied, make your move and duck into the dressing room.

3 | Have your partner follow behind a few minutes later.

4 | Be quiet.
The walls to dressing rooms are thin.

5 | Be quick.
Speed is important, especially if your legs are visible beneath the walls.

6 | Depart from the dressing room one person at a time. Check your appearance in the mirror, and leave the store's clothes in the dressing room. If you are in the women's section of a department store, the woman should leave first and make sure the coast is clear. If you are in the men's department, the man should leave first.

Be Aware
For speed and efficiency in airplanes, elevators, and dressing rooms, be sure to wear loose, baggy clothing. Do not wear underwear.

HOW TO MAKE YOUR ONLINE PROFILE MORE ALLURING

1 Post a flattering photograph.
Pose with children or animals.

2 Use euphemisms.
For instance, avoid the word "unemployed" by saying that you are currently enjoying a sweat-free lifestyle while you search for a new challenge.

3 Seem rich.
Refer to signs of affluence such as luxury brands, cruises, vacations, and resorts in exotic locales.

4 Seem interesting.
Discuss a variety of interesting hobbies such as rock climbing, photography, and wine.

5 Seem cultured.
List "favorites" that present you as educated and sophisticated, yet not pretentious. Mention highbrow and mainstream books, movies, TV shows, and musicians to create the impression that you have eclectic and wide-ranging taste.

6 Keep it positive.
Avoid mention of a breakup.

Post a flattering photograph. Pose with children or animals.

PERSONAL AD PHOTO DECODER

Photo Posted for Online Personal Ad	What it Says about You
Photos with an ex-girlfriend	I have been on a date before.
High school yearbook photos	I am 20 pounds heavier than this.
Party photos	I am drunk right now.
Baby photo	I was cute a long time ago.
Arrest "mug" shots	I will stalk you if we break up.
You with stuffed animals	I will stalk you if we break up.
Altered pictures of you with celebrities	I live in my parents' basement.
Wedding photos	I am married.
Nude photos	I am desperate.

PICKUP LINES TO AVOID

The human body is 90 percent water, and I'm real thirsty.

Can I buy you a drink or do you just want the money?

With a mane like that you must be a Leo.

Do you have a mirror in your pants? Because I can see myself in them.

Are your legs tired? Because you have been running through my dreams all night.

Is your father a thief? He has stolen the stars from the skies and put them in your eyes.

Are you okay? It must have been a long fall from heaven.

I really like that outfit. It would look great crumpled at the end of my bed.

What do you like to eat for breakfast? Oh good, I have that.

I know they say milk does a body good—but damn, how much have you been drinking?

So, are you legal?

I have cable TV.

If I told you that you have a lovely body, would you hold it against me?

Did the sun just come out or did you smile at me?

Is it hot in here, or is it just you?

Do you believe in love at first sight or do I have to walk by you again?

Hey, I lost my phone number . . . can I have yours?

If you were a burger at McDonald's, I'd call you McBeautiful.

Hi, my name's _____. But you can call me . . . tonight.

No wonder the sky's gray today—all the blue is in your eyes.

What's your name? Or shall I just call you mine?

If I could rearrange the alphabet, I'd put U and I together.

Look at you with all those curves and me with
no brakes!

I may not be Fred Flintstone/Wilma Flintstone, but
I can sure make your bed rock!

Do you have any raisins? No? How about a date?

Do you have a Band-Aid? 'Cause I skinned my knee
when I fell for you.

Can I have a picture of you so I can show Santa what
I want for Christmas?

My bed is broken. Can I sleep in yours?

I'm not feeling myself tonight. Can I feel you?

My name is _____. Remember that; you'll
be screaming it later.

Is that a ladder in your stockings or the stairway
to heaven?

I may not be the best looking guy/girl in here, but
I'm the only one talking to you.

(Lick finger and wipe on his/her shirt.) Let's get you
out of these wet clothes.

HOW TO END A RELATIONSHIP

1 Get out immediately.

The moment you realize you are in—or starting to get into—a relationship that is not working for you, just say "no."

2 Decide on a mode of communication.

Voicemail, e-mail, or a card may be considered cowardly. However, these options have their advantages, particularly for a short-term relationship. If you are ending a long-term relationship, consider drafting a letter as a way to begin a conversation. Hand it to your partner to read while you are there.

3 Be kind.

Mention the things you like about your partner and express gratitude for the good times you have had together. This may seem contrived, but do it anyway.

4 State your position simply.

Be decisive, leaving no room for doubt or negotiation. It is not necessary for the other person to agree with you or to understand your reasons, but try to explain. One of the consequences of terminating a relationship is that you no longer have to get the other person to understand or agree.

5 Keep the focus on yourself.

Talk only about yourself, not the other person: Don't make it their fault. Say something simple and true, such as, "I prefer not to continue dating, but I want you to know how much I have enjoyed your sense of humor," or, "This relationship just is not working for me." If necessary, repeat these phrases.

6 Do not belabor the point.

You do not need to go over all the advantages and disadvantages of the relationship. Do not offer critical feedback or long explanations. If your real reason for breaking up might be painful for the other person to hear, do not mention it.

7 Do not try to take away the pain.

You are doing what is right for you and the other person has a right to a response. It is no longer your job to make the person feel better. Be firm but not cruel.

8 Never say, "I will call you."

When tossed out insincerely, this phrase is unimaginative and unkind. Instead, try saying something more honest and more final: "Maybe we will see each other again sometime. If not, have a nice life."

BREAKUP TEXTS

4GET IT	TTYN
C U NVR	ITS OVR
H8 U	MOVD ON
UR DUMPT	U & I R DUN
NO LUV U NO MO	BEAT IT
U SUK	U R NOW EX

HOW TO LIVE WITH AN EX UNTIL ONE OF YOU MOVES OUT

⭐ Divide the apartment.
Affix tape to the floor. Move all belongings to appropriate side. Hang drapes or sheets around your space to create the feeling of separate rooms.

⭐ Arrange a board in the center of the bed.
Divide pillows evenly.

⭐ Label food.
Claim sides of the refrigerator.

⭐ Cut your couple pictures in half.
Return to appropriate parties.

⭐ Divvy up antidepressants in the medicine cabinet.

⭐ Schedule custody of the shared pet.
Draw up a timetable that clearly outlines when each of you is allotted time with Spot.

⭐ Arrange for two entrances.
Take turns entering and exiting the apartment through the fire escape.

⭐ Communicate via sticky notes.

Divide the apartment to create the feeling of separate rooms.

SIGNS YOU'RE NOT OVER YOUR EX

- You accidentally call anyone you are dating by your ex's name.
- Your new relationship is with your old "safety."
- You call your ex's roommate regularly.
- You make lunch dates with your ex's mother.
- You sob uncontrollably when you hear "your song."
- Your social networking status is still "taken."
- You call her when you're drunk.
- You call her when you're sober.
- You check her online photo-sharing account hourly for updates.
- You are still planning the wedding.
- You sleep with her picture.
- You are parked outside of her house.

HOW TO MAKE YOUR BETROTHED'S PARENTS LIKE YOU

⭐ **Be direct.**
Have a conversation about your feelings. Start with, "I've noticed a change in our relationship, and I was wondering if I have done something to offend." Talk about the issue from your point of view. Use phrases such as "I feel this" as opposed to "you did this" so they will not feel attacked. Listen carefully and remain open to criticism.

⭐ **Be nice.**
Remain pleasant and respectful, and you will eventually wear them down. Be patient, as this might take some time.

⭐ **Arrange for testimonials.**
Ask friends, relatives, and neighbors to vouch for your value as a human being when your future in-laws come to visit. Leave information packets on their pillows that include letters of recommendation from coaches, employers, teachers, and religious and community leaders. Include a pie chart that expresses the amount of time you devote each day to your future spouse.

★ Volunteer your services.

Help with household tasks such as changing the kitty litter, caulking the tub, or walking the dog at the crack of dawn. Take them to the airport at rush hour, teach your betrothed's younger siblings how to drive, install their new computer system, repoint the brick exterior of their home, prepare their tax returns, refinish the floors throughout their house, and detail their car.

★ Find a common bond.

If your in-laws dislike you because they do not know you, invite them out together or separately on outings they enjoy. If your mother-in-law likes tea, ask her to tea. If she prefers the theater, take her to a play. Take your father-in-law golfing, or if he's a man of few words, to the movies or a nightclub. Pick up the tab.

★ Plant a diary where your in-laws will be sure to find it.

Fill the diary with virtuous thoughts and aspirations. Declare your love for your betrothed repeatedly. Add entries about how much you like your future in-laws and how much you hope they'll like you, too.

★ Pretend you are friends with celebrities.

Find out who their heroes are (politicians, authors, activists, sports figures, movie stars, etc.) and autograph and frame a glossy photo of a celebrity to yourself. Mention to your future in-laws you might be able to pull a few strings if they'd like to meet the famous person.

★ Pay for the wedding.
If you or your family are already paying for the wedding, offer to pay off their mortgage or car payments.

★ Let them move in.
Give them the big bathroom.

★ Promise to provide them with a grandchild within a negotiated period of time.

HOW TO SURVIVE THE BACHELOR PARTY

How to Pick a Lock (When Handcuffed to a Bowling Ball)

A classic bachelor party prank uses a bowling ball and handcuffs to translate literally the expression "the old ball and chain."

1 Locate a pick.
A handcuff lock can be picked relatively easily with a piece of metal bent into the shape of a key. Whatever you use, the material must be resilient because the springs on a handcuff lock are strong. Use any of the following items:
- Mini screwdriver
- Large paper clip
- Any tough wire (e.g., chicken or piano)
- Small fork
- Hairpin

2 Bend a few millimeters of one end of your pick 90 degrees.

3 Insert the pick into the lock.
Fit the bend into the lock at the point where the nipple of the key fits. You will feel the bend move into place.

4 Turn the pick to open the lock.

Turn the pick left and then right. If the pick won't move, put the latch end of the handcuff vertically on a hard surface and press down. This may relieve a bit of pressure off the lock and make it easier to turn. Be careful, though: Pushing too hard may lock the cuff another tooth and restrict your hand movement.

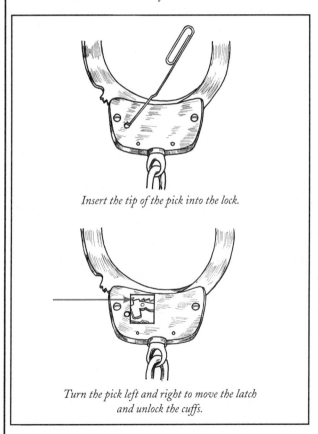

Insert the tip of the pick into the lock.

Turn the pick left and right to move the latch and unlock the cuffs.

How to Smoke a Cigar

1 Clip the head.
The head, or smoking end, of the cigar is covered by a small area of leaf called the cap. Using a sharp cigar cutter, quickly make a guillotine cut, removing a small section (¼ inch or less) of the cap. Do not cut below the end of the cap, or the wrapper may come apart. If no cigar cutter is available, punch a hole in the cap using the tip of a pen or pencil.

2 Hold the cigar in your nondominant hand.

3 Ignite a torch lighter or a long wooden match.
Do not put the cigar to your lips.

4 Toast the end.
Carefully move the flame to the foot (end) while rotating the cigar slowly. This will ensure an even burn. The foot should ignite thoroughly and evenly.

5 When the foot is lit, bring the cigar to your lips.

6 Draw smoke into your mouth.
Suck the smoke through the cigar slowly and evenly while still holding the flame an inch or two from the foot.

7 Puff gently until the foot is completely lit.
Do not inhale the smoke into your lungs.

8 Exhale.

Savor the flavor of the cigar in your mouth for a few seconds before expelling the smoke.

9 Repeat steps 7 and 8.

Take one or two draws from the cigar per minute, but do not rush. Rotate the cigar slowly in your fingers or allow it to sit in an ashtray between draws. Keep the foot elevated to maintain an even burn. Avoid squeezing the cigar.

10 Flick the ash.

Allow half an inch to an inch of ash to accumulate on the foot. Tap the cigar gently with a finger to make the ash fall. Many cigar smokers will try to get the ash as long as possible before flicking it. However, you should flick the ash if you feel it is about to fall and burn a hole in clothing or furniture.

11 Extinguish the cigar.

Many smokers will discard a cigar when half to three-quarters has been smoked. A quality cigar may be smoked as long as its flavor is still pleasing and the smoke is cool enough to be comfortable in your mouth.

Be Aware

- A *natural*—a cigar with a light brown wrapper—is mild and is more appropriate for beginners. (A *maduro*, or a cigar with a dark brown wrapper, will be rich and full flavored, but may be too harsh for a novice smoker.)

- The wrapper should not be dry, flaking, or crack when handled.
- Gently squeeze the cigar. It should be firm and give lightly to the touch, then regain its shape. A moist cigar has been overhumidified and will not draw well.
- While it may be socially frowned upon, a cigar may be extinguished and relit. Scoop or blow all carbon from the foot of the cigar before relighting, or cut the cigar just above the burned section.

HOW TO FIX
WEDDING ATTIRE

Tux Too Small

⭐ Swap tuxedos.
If your tuxedo matches the style of those worn by the groomsmen or waiter, exchange yours for one that fits: It is better for a groomsman or waiter to look poorly dressed than the groom.

⭐ Expand the waistband.
Make a chain of two or three safety pins, depending on how much additional room is required. Secure the sides of the waistband together using pins. Your cummerbund will hide the fix. Do not remove the cummerbund during the wedding.

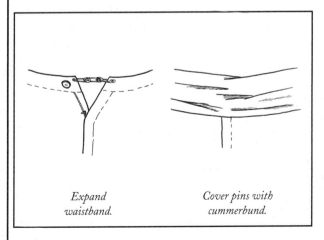

*Expand
waistband.*

*Cover pins with
cummerbund.*

✪ **Replace the pants.**
Locate a pair of black pants that fit. Cut a piece of black electrical tape the same length as the pant leg, waist to hem. Cut the tape in half lengthwise. Affix one half on the side seam of the right leg of the pants. Repeat for your left leg.

✪ **Keep the jacket unbuttoned.**
Buttoning the jacket will make the improper fit more apparent.

✪ **Distract with your cufflinks.**
If the jacket sleeves are too short, make sure your cufflinks are of a high quality. Keep your arms slightly bent at all times to reduce the obviousness of the length disparity.

✪ **Expand the shirt collar.**
Loop a rubber band through the buttonhole of the shirt collar. Secure the ends to the collar button. Conceal with a necktie. Do not remove the tie during the wedding.

SPLIT SEAM

1 Remove the jacket, shirt, or pants.

2 Turn the garment inside out.

3 Pull the seam together.
There will be a narrow section of fabric behind the

seam. Pull the split sections together. Line up the sides carefully.

4 | Pin.
Using safety pins, connect the two sides. Pin the material as close to the seam as possible, but not so close that the pins will be visible from the outside.

5 | Check the repair.
Turn the garment right-side out. If the seam holds and the pins are not visible, the repair was successful. If the pins are visible, remove and start over.

Be Aware

If no safety pins are available, use staples. Take care when removing them to prevent rips in the fabric. If neither pins nor staples are available, use electrical or duct tape. Fast-drying glue is also effective for repairing torn garments, but may damage or stain the fabric.

LOST BOW TIE

Make an emergency replacement from a cloth napkin.
- Place a well-starched white dinner napkin flat on a table in front of you. Using a pencil, carefully draw a circle about one inch in diameter.
- To the left of the circle, draw a triangle with sides about two inches long. One point of the triangle should extend slightly into the circle.

how to fix wedding attire

• Repeat, drawing a second triangle to the right of the circle, with one point extending into the circle. Your drawing should look like a bow tie when viewed from the front.

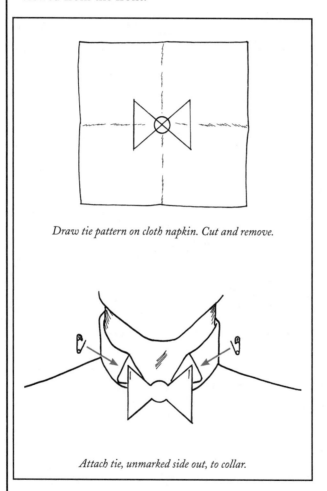

Draw tie pattern on cloth napkin. Cut and remove.

Attach tie, unmarked side out, to collar.

- Use scissors to cut the bow tie from the napkin. Turn the bow tie over so the pencil marks are on the back.
- Secure the cutout to your collar using loops of tape or safety pins. Do not wear with a black cummerbund; make an emergency napkin cummerbund (see page 230) to match.

Wear a medallion.

Open your shirt at the collar and open three additional buttons. For a more fashionable look, borrow a spread collar shirt (one without a wing collar, which is made for a bow tie). Borrow and wear a large medallion, gold cross, Star of David, giant locket, or flashy pendant. To make a medallion:

- Open a wedding gift wrapped in gold-colored wrapping paper.
- Wrap the gold paper around a drink coaster or a similar-sized piece of cardboard. Cut the paper to fit, then tape or glue to cover.
- Affix your medallion to a black dress shoelace or piece of string with tape.
- Hang around your neck.

Make a bolo tie.
- Thread a black shoelace (leather or nylon) under and around your shirt collar to simulate a bolo lanyard.
- Run the two loose ends through the backing of a pin, pendant, or horizontal tie clasp.
- Slide the clasp up so it sits just below the second shirt button. Keep your collar button open.

EMERGENCY CUFF LINKS

1 Remove your shirt.

2 Thread a narrow (⅛- to ¼-inch-wide) ribbon through the cuff holes.
Leave the cuff open about half an inch. Do not tie the ends.

3 Tie knots.
On the outside of one cuff, tie a small knot on the ribbon as close to the hole as possible. Tie a second knot on top of the first.

4 Check the knot diameter.
Test the knot by pulling gently on the other end of the ribbon. If the knot pulls through easily, tie another knot on top of the first two.

5 Trim the ends.
When the knot is too big to fit through the hole easily, snip the excess ribbon just past the knot. Repeat on the other side of the cuff, then on the other sleeve. The knots may be pushed through the cuff holes after the shirt is on. They will hold the cuffs closed and look similar to braided silk cuff knots.

Be Aware
• Keep the jacket sleeve pulled down as far as possible to hide an unsightly fix.

Emergency Cuff Links

shoelace

cherry stem

twist tie

- Items that can be used as emergency cuff links:
  - paper clips
  - twist ties
  - rubber bands
  - the metal rings from two key chains
  - large earrings
  - Maraschino cherry stems tied in knots
  - shoelaces (cut short)

EMERGENCY CUMMERBUND

You will need a white cloth napkin for a white-tie wedding or a black or dark blue napkin for a black-tie event, plus a couple additional napkins to secure the cummerbund. The napkins should be starched and slightly stiff.

1 Place the napkin flat on a table in front of you, with one corner pointing toward you.

2 Fold the corner closest to you and the opposite corner into the center of the napkin.

3 Fold the bottom half of the napkin up toward the top edge.
The bottom edge should be about one inch above the top edge when the fold is complete.

4 Fold both upper edges down toward the bottom edge. The lower of the two pleats should be one inch above the bottom edge. The napkin should now have three

pleats and be the approximate shape of a cummerbund.

5 Secure.
Tightly roll another napkin on the diagonal so it is
long and thin. Tie or pin the second (or two more)
napkin(s) to one end of the cummerbund, run it
around your back, then tie or pin it to the other end.
The pleats of the cummerbund should face up. Your
jacket will obscure the sides of the napkin, even when
unbuttoned.

Prevent Perspiration Stains from Showing

★ Wear an undershirt.
A thin cotton T-shirt will absorb sweat before it
reaches your exterior layer of clothing.

★ Wear perspiration shields.
Tape several layers of tissue paper, paper towels, or
cocktail napkins to the underarm area on the inside of
your shirt to absorb excess wetness. Do not use colored
tissue or napkins because the ink from the dye may
stain your shirt when wet.

★ Wear chamois.
Cut a piece of chamois cloth, the ultra-absorbent cloth
often employed for drying and polishing cars, into two
4-inch squares. Tape the squares to the underarm area
on the inside of your shirt to remain extra dry.

★ Wear a pantiliner.

Apply a self-sticking pantiliner or other feminine product to the underarm area on the inside of the shirt. Make sure you remove the product in private before joining your new spouse after the wedding.

Be Aware

If you discover that the sweat has come through and is visible on your shirt, use a blow-dryer or hot-air hand dryer to dry the wet areas. It is not necessary to remove the shirt first.

HOW TO SURVIVE THE FIRST DANCE AT YOUR WEDDING

If you have two left feet, the first dance at your wedding can be awkward.

1 Warm up.
Get comfortable moving together. Before the first dance, find a quiet space and move around the room in sync. Hold hands and move together in simple side to side and back and forth steps.

2 Dim the lights.

3 Tell the band leader to keep it short.
Inform the band of the name of your song and that you want it to end quickly. Two minutes are plenty.

4 Hold each other.
Lean lightly into your partner from the center of your body. Keep your knees soft. The groom should place his hand on the bride's shoulder blade with his fingers parallel to the floor. The bride should place her hand on the groom's right shoulder. The couple's arms should maintain contact. Make sure your legs are offset so that each foot has its own "track" to move along. The groom's chin should line up with the bride's right shoulder.

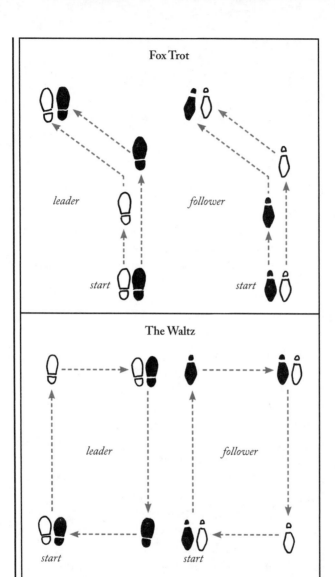

Fox Trot

leader

follower

start

start

The Waltz

leader

follower

start

start

5 Do not rush.
When the music starts, sway from side to side for a moment to feel the music. Then, on the beat, begin.

6 Attempt a basic fox trot or waltz.
See diagrams for each step on opposite page.

7 Whisper and laugh.
Appear to be conversing, enjoying yourselves, and joking. People will assume any missteps are the result of merriment rather than poor dancing ability.

8 Distract the audience with a dip.
A flashy dip will focus attention on what you can do instead of what you cannot. The groom should rotate the bride sideways rather than leaning over her in the dip, both to increase the drama and for increased safety. The bride should not give the groom her entire body weight to support, and he should not dip the bride so deeply that she cannot engage her abdominal muscles to support herself.

9 Arrange for someone to cut in.
Have the bride's father and the groom's mother cut in after 30 seconds, or fewer if you are severely challenged.

Be Aware

- Apply petroleum jelly to the surface of the instep of men's patent leather shoes so they will glide if they make contact.
- If you get rattled and lose the beat, recover by moving from side to side for a few moments until you both recover.
- Select a fast-tempo dance so you don't have to move together.
- Do not tango.

HOW TO SURVIVE IF YOU FORGET HER BIRTHDAY

1 Apologize. Apologize. Apologize.
Your apology might have to take several forms—flowers, verbal protestations, love letters, a special dinner. Be creative.

2 Accept responsibility for your error.
Recognize sincerely that you blew it. Excuses will only make things worse.

3 Acknowledge her feelings.
Accept your partner's anger as valid and do not question or challenge any reaction. Say, "I can only begin to imagine how you must feel."

4 Plan a special event to fix the mistake.
A weekend getaway, a night at a fancy hotel, or an extremely thoughtful gift will be necessary. However, do not show up two days late with a windfall of gifts, expecting that all will be forgiven. All the presents in the world cannot eliminate the need for talking the matter through.

How to Survive If You Forget Your Anniversary

⭐ Order an emergency bouquet.
Many florists can assemble arrangements with little notice. If you have just minutes to prepare, scour your neighborhood flowerbeds for daisies. Wrap them in colorful ribbon and present them as your initial gift.

⭐ Buy chocolates.
Most supermarkets and drugstores carry chocolate assortments. Choose a tasteful boxed set rather than several loose candy bars tied with ribbon.

⭐ Create a voucher card.
Prepare a card or piece of paper that shows the wonderful gift you're giving but can't give now because it isn't ready yet. Draw a picture of the gift on the card or paper.

⭐ Apologize, apologize, apologize.
If you're caught with nothing, making excuses will not help your case. Your level of contrition should be so extreme that your spouse begins to feel bad because you feel so terrible.

⭐ Give an intangible present.
Give her a homemade certificate for a weekend spa getaway. It could be for her only, or for a romantic weekend for both of you.

THINGS BACHELORS DON'T HAVE TO DO

- Buy vegetables
- Vacuum
- Buy anything "lite"
- Buy wine coolers
- Drink diet soda
- Stock the freezer with frozen yogurt
- Watch sports on mute
- Put down the toilet seat
- Hang up towels
- Do laundry
- Wipe hair out of the sink
- Belch quietly
- Clean
- Eat at the kitchen table
- Make the bed
- Watch the Lifetime channel
- Drink out of glasses
- Host dinner parties
- Get out of bed before noon

CHAPTER 4

DOMESTIC DISASTERS

GARAGE EMERGENCIES

Box Avalanche

⭐ Duck and cover your head with your arms and curl into a ball on the floor.
If a shelf has fallen toward you, stay as close to the shelf/wall as possible to avoid being hit by objects falling out as well as down.

Box Stuck in Rafters

⭐ Set an extension ladder under the rafter.
Climb up, and hand the box down to someone below if it is full of heavy materials. If the box is light and the contents aren't fragile, place a mattress on the floor and knock the box down with a telescoping lightbulb changer or two brooms held together with duct tape.

Bats Living in Garage

⭐ Turn on a bright light.
Leave the light on all night, several nights in a row. The bats will leave of their own accord.

Carbon Monoxide Buildup

⭐ Do not enter the garage.
Open the garage door with a remote opener to vent

the gas. If the garage must be opened manually, open the door from the outside. Open any side doors if it is possible to do so without entering the garage. Wait 10 to 15 minutes, enter the garage, and turn off the car engine.

Garage Door Closes on Car

✪ **Stop the car immediately.**
For a manual garage door, pull up on the handle and move the door to its fully open position. Electric garage door openers manufactured after 1993 should—if they haven't malfunctioned—have sensors that prevent the door from closing on a person or object and automatically reverse the door to its fully open position when it strikes something.

Missing Tool

✪ **Think back to the last time you had visual or physical contact with the tool.**
Revisit the locations of major or minor tasks that may have involved the tool. If you believe the tool has been borrowed but not returned, confront potential suspects, including your children, spouse, relatives, and neighbors. If the suspect denies having possession of the tool, conduct an independent search of the suspect's room, car, home, yard, or garage. If the search is unsuccessful, ask to borrow, or simply borrow, a tool or item of equal value.

garage emergencies

How to Escape If Stuck Under a Car

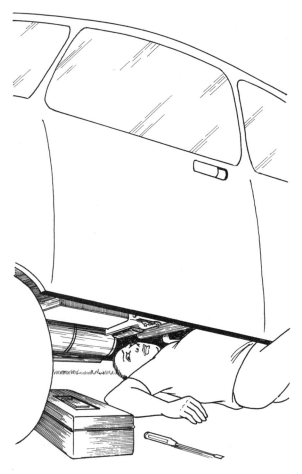

Suck in your gut, grasp the edge of the undercarriage of the car, and pull to drag yourself free. If you cannot hold in your gut for the length of extrication, suck in and pull or push toward the edge of car in small stages until free.

HOW TO MAKE HOUSEHOLD CHORES FUN

⭐ Raise the stakes.
Pretend you are a secret agent. Imagine that if you do not finish washing, drying, and folding laundry within one hour, a large city will be destroyed.

⭐ Make it a drinking game.
Award yourself a beer or shot for every dish washed, toilet cleaned, etc.

⭐ Do a play-by-play.
Offer an ongoing description of your actions as you perform them. "And he's reaching for the cord of the lawnmower—he's pulling it, and pulling it, and—he's got it! The mower is on!"

⭐ Do the chores in the middle of the night.
Pretend you are a ninja or a burglar, and you must complete the chores in total silence or risk discovery.

⭐ Put on music.
Find music that enlivens the chore-doing drudgery (hip-hop) rather than exacerbates it (funeral marches).

⭐ Bribe your kids to do your chores.
Offer them candy or a trip to the toy store.

HOW TO SURVIVE
A COCKROACH
INFESTATION

1 Rid your kitchen of any food residue.
Thoroughly scour the kitchen counters, dining table, stovetops, and any other areas where food is prepared or consumed. Remove all food from the kitchen and clean inside all cabinets and drawers. Empty, rinse, and scrub every trash can. Clean the refrigerator inside and out, the underside of the microwave, and the crumb tray of the toaster.

2 Clean the rest of your apartment.
Pull out sofa pillows and vacuum away any crumbs using a crack-and-crevice attachment; roll up all carpets and sweep and mop the floor underneath.

3 Dry your apartment.
Look for puddles underneath the sink, around the base of the bathtub, and next to the toilet. At each sink, turn on both taps and, as the water is running, examine the base of the faucet, the tap handle, and the underside of the sink. Tighten the joints and recaulk any areas of seepage. Repeat this procedure with the taps in the bath.

Eat out instead of cooking in your home.

4 Eliminate roach hideouts.

Get down on all fours and crawl from room to room, carefully examining each pantry, closet, drawer, and cupboard. Destroy any potential roach hiding places, such as bags stuffed with other bags, piles of old magazines, or cardboard boxes waiting to be recycled. Open old boxes, take out their contents, flatten the cardboard, and remove from your apartment.

5 Place "survey traps" in ten sites around your apartment.
Position "sticky traps" throughout the apartment. Place each trap against a wall or corner, under a sink, or along the baseboards.

6 Monitor the traps.
Carefully note the number of dead roaches in each trap to determine where in your apartment the roaches are most prevalent.

7 Kill the roaches with borax.
Mix 4 parts borax with 2 parts flour and 1 part cocoa powder. Sprinkle liberally in roach-heavy areas of your apartment.

8 Maintain a clean, dry apartment.
After each meal, thoroughly clean the areas where food was cooked and consumed. Store all food in sealed containers. Do all dishes immediately. Take out any garbage and recycling at least once a day. Make sure to immediately clean up any water spills and repair leaky faucets. Whenever possible, eat out instead of cooking in your home; do not bring home leftovers.

9 Convince your neighbors to keep equally clean.

Be Aware
Read the sticky trap instructions carefully, especially if you have pets and/or children.

SIGNS OF A ROACH INFESTATION	
Roach droppings	Small clusters of black, ridged pellets measuring ⅛-inch.
Gastrointestinal problems	Potential ailments include diarrhea, vomiting, and dysentery. Caused by organisms transferred from the arms and legs of cockroaches onto food and utensils.
Allergic responses	Symptoms include watery eyes, skin rashes, sneezing, and congested nasal passages. Caused by the presence of roach droppings and molted roach skin in the air.
Cockroach sightings	The most common cockroach in New York is the German cockroach, which is a tan or light brown winged insect, measuring from ½ to 1 inch, with two dark streaks down its back. You may find roaches: *in the kitchen, or any area with abundant food *in the bathroom, or anywhere there is standing water *in or near the garbage or recycling

how to survive a cockroach infestation

HOW TO SHARE A STUDIO APARTMENT WITH THREE ROOMMATES

⭐ Put everything in writing.
Before all roommates move in, create a roommates contract (see page 252).

⭐ Label all possessions.
Put your name on your food, books, CDs, portable electronic devices, clothing, and pets. Nothing, including food, should be considered "communal property," unless explicitly agreed upon by all roommates in the contract.

⭐ Utilize feng shui.
Minimize clutter, decorate with bright colors, and hang numerous mirrors to maximize the feeling of openness and harmony. Store or throw away any possessions that are unnecessary. As many furniture items as possible should be designated "multiuse": futon pulls out into bed, ottoman turns into night table, bathtub with plank of wood across it becomes desk.

⭐ Subdivide.
Place a bookcase in the middle of the space to give the illusion of multiple rooms; repeat several times

until the apartment is divided into several tiny mini-apartments. Hang framed signs at the entrance to each "room," with titles such as "Bob's Room," "Allison's Room," and "the parlor." Put tape on the floor to demarcate various territories and provide directions.

Subdivide the room into several tiny mini-apartments.

★ Communicate.

Convene weekly roommate meetings to maintain an ongoing dialogue. Each roommate should keep a notebook to write down things that are bothering him. Share complaints and positive support at the weekly meeting. Encourage all roommates to use "I" statements to express their feelings in a calm, nonconfrontational manner.

ROOMMATES CONTRACT

- A rotating chore schedule for undesirable communal responsibilities: cleaning the toilet, taking out the garbage and recycling. Specify individual responsibilities: doing laundry, walking your dog, washing dishes, watering the plants.

- Financial obligations: who pays for what and in what proportion, including heat/electric/gas, rent, maintenance-related costs, and any shared food.

- A schedule for sharing communal resources: shower, kitchen, TV. If there are not enough beds or sofas for every person to have one, specify who gets to sleep at what times—and rotate.

HOW TO TREAT A SHAVING WOUND

MINOR CUT

1 Rinse the cut with clean, cold water.

2 Apply alum salts or talcum powder.
Alum, a mineral sometimes sold as styptic powder or a styptic pencil, stops blood flow. Hold the alum in place for 10 to 20 seconds, depending on the severity of the wound. While effective, this technique can be painful, since it is literally applying "salt to the wound." The quickly dried cut may also form a noticeable scab. Alternatively, apply a liberal coating of talcum powder to the cut. Although slightly messier than alum, talcum is considerably less painful and will conceal the nicks and cuts.

If alum or talcum powder is not available, proceed to step 3.

3 Apply toilet paper.
Tear off a tiny piece of toilet paper or tissue and press it onto the cut for at least 15 seconds, until it adheres by itself.

4 Wait a few minutes.

5 Remove the toilet paper.

Moisten the paper before carefully pulling it from the cut. If it is not moistened, the paper may reopen the cut when you peel it off.

Major Laceration

Most serious shaving wounds occur to the neck, underneath the nose, or underneath an earlobe. The steps below focus on a neck laceration, but can apply to a major wound anywhere.

1 Apply firm pressure directly over the wound.

Place your fingertips at the point where the bleeding seems to be most severe.

2 If the bleeding stops, continue the pressure for an additional 10 minutes.

Remain still until the bleeding subsides. Then go to an emergency room.

3 If the bleeding does not stop, do not panic.

You probably have slowed the flow enough to have time for the next steps.

4 Pinch and hold the bleeding area.

Use your dominant thumb and index finger to pinch the skin where the blood flow is coming from. This will most likely close the vessel even if you cannot see it and will stop the serious bleeding.

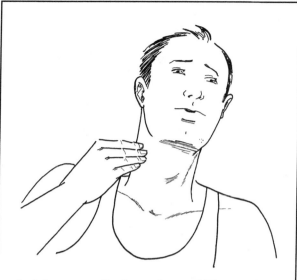

Apply firm pressure directly over the wound. Place your finger-tips at the point where the bleeding seems to be most severe.

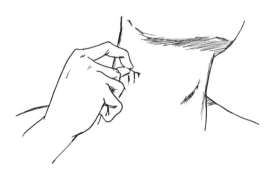

Pushing above or below the site will help seal the area where blood vessels enter the wound.

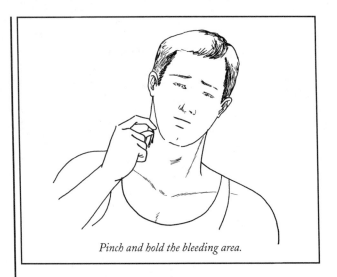

Pinch and hold the bleeding area.

5 | Locate the bleeding vessel.

If the bleeding continues despite the steps above, use a piece of cloth or tissue to help you find the exact location of the cut vessel. Carefully ease off the finger pressure while wiping blood away from the wound with the cloth. This should make it easier to see the end of the cut vessel, or to pinpoint its location even if it is deep under the skin. When you see it, try pinching it again.

6 | Apply pressure directly above and below the bleeding site.

If bleeding is still profuse, maintain finger pressure over the wound while pushing immediately above and below the bleeding site. This will seal the areas where blood vessels enter the wound.

7 | Get to an emergency room.

If you are being driven to the emergency room, recline with your head raised slightly. Keep firm pressure on the wound even if the bleeding seems to slow.

Be Aware

- If the blood flows in a steady stream, you have hit a vein and can block the blood flow by pressing above the wound. If the blood is spurting, you have lacerated an artery and can block the blood flow by pressing (hard) below the wound. (See step 6.)

- There are four jugular veins. The external jugulars, paired on the right and left sides of the neck, are vulnerable because they lie right under the surface of the skin. The internal jugulars, also paired, lie close to the center of the neck front, but are about an inch under the skin in a protective sheath. If you accidentally cut your neck razor-shaving and notice a great deal of bleeding, you've probably cut the external jugular.

FACIAL HAIR OPTIONS

The 1970s Detective

The Man of Mystery

The God

The Son of God

The Abraham Lincoln

The Grover Cleveland

FACIAL HAIR OPTIONS

The Mark Twain

The Charles Dickens

The Muttonchops

The Superchops

The Soul Patch

*The Too Much Time
on Your Hands*

HOW TO TIE A TIE

HALF-WINDSOR KNOT

1 Drape and position the tie.

Standing before a full-length mirror, hang the tie over your neck so that when you look at yourself in the mirror, you see the fat side on the right, and the skinny side on the left, front sides facing the mirror. Tug down on the fat end until it hangs a foot below the bottom of the skinny end.

2 Cross over.

Bring the fat end across the front of the skinny end and wrap around the skinny end so that you can now see the back side (label and stitching visible) of the fat end in the mirror.

3 Lift and tuck.

Lift the fat end toward your face (label side will be facing you) and tuck into and pull it through the loop of the tie at your Adam's apple. The fat end of the tie will now be resting against your chest, label side visible in the mirror.

4 Bring it around the front.

Take the wide fat end and pass it in front of the skinny end, from right to left (label side will be facing your chest).

5 | Bring it up and over.
Slip the fat end under the loop of the tie around your neck. The label side will be facing the mirror and the front of the tie will be in front of your face.

6 | Tuck and tighten.
Slip the fat end of the tie face-side out through the knot at your Adam's apple and carefully tug the knot closed to draw it up to your collar. The skinny end should not be visible and lie underneath the fat end. Use the mirror to check and adjust the tie at your neck so that it is not visible at the back of your collar.

Bow Tie

1 | Drape the tie.
Hang the tie over your neck so that the left side hangs about 1½ inches lower than the right.

2 | Cross the left end over the right, then bring the left end through the loop.
Bring the longer hanging end (the one on the left) over the right, then pull it up towards your face, through the little hole at your neck that you've created.

3 | Fold the other end inwards.
Fold the shorter hanging end in half, and align it with the points of your shirt collar.

4 | Bring the long end down over the center.
Bring the longer end down, so it hangs over the front of the now doubled-over short end.

5 | Bring the long end up from behind, and double it over.
Grasp the longer hanging end with your forefinger, and bring it up behind the short end; as you bring it up, fold it over itself.

6 | Poke through the opening behind the loop.
Take the folded-over long end and poke it through the knot behind the front loop. You now should have two loops coming from either side of the center hole. Tug on either side until the bow is neat and straight.

HOW TO PREVENT SNORING

★ **Change sleep positions.**
Snoring is often caused by lying on your back. Train yourself to sleep on your side or stomach.

★ **Sew a tennis ball to the back of your pajamas.**
Prevent yourself from turning over onto your back in the middle of the night by attaching a tennis ball to your back. This will force you to lie on your side, effectively ridding you of the habit.

★ **Avoid alcohol.**
Alcohol and other sedatives increase muscle relaxation, which increases snoring.

★ **Change your diet.**
Reduce the amount of refined carbohydrates and dairy products that you consume. Both increase mucus production which can cause snoring. Also avoid eating large meals at night right before bed.

★ **Exercise.**
Extra body fat, especially bulky neck tissue, can cause snoring. Losing just 10 percent of your body weight can improve your overall breathing.

★ **Apply nasal strips.**
Open nasal passages with adhesive nose strips.

Sew a tennis ball to the back of your pajamas.

⭐ **Use a throat spray.**
Lubricate your throat with a spray that will relax the throat muscles.

★ Practice aromatherapy.
Reduce nasal congestion with essential oils. Leave a jar of marjoram oil open on your nightstand while you sleep. Add a few drops of eucalyptus oil to a water-filled humidifier. Breathe in the steam just prior to going to bed.

★ Use a neti pot.
Reduce allergens in your sinuses by washing out your nasal passages with a neti pot. Fill the pot with water and ¼ teaspoon of salt. Hold your head over a sink at an angle so your chin is parallel with your forehead. Tilt the pot so the tip of the arm enters one nostril. Allow the water to flow in one nostril and out the other. Repeat in the other nostril.

★ Prop up your mattress.
Put a dictionary, encyclopedia, or phone book under your mattress to raise your head and change the angle of your neck.

HOW TO APOLOGIZE WHEN YOU DON'T KNOW WHAT YOU'VE DONE WRONG

1 | Evaluate the threat level.
Examine your partner's pupils and nostrils. Pupils dilated/nostrils flared means that you are in an extreme amount of trouble. If the pupils are not dilated, and nostrils are not flared, make a small silly joke or offer a nonsexual compliment and see if a smile is offered. An apology may not be required.

2 | Do not guess.
Do not panic and start apologizing for things which your partner may not in fact be aware of. By saying, "I am sorry I was late paying the mortgage," when she may not have known that, may put you in twice as much trouble as before.

3 | Offer a nonspecific apology.
"I'm sorry for what I did. What I did was bad. It was a dumb thing to do."

4 | Offer a nonspecific excuse.
"I had a lot on my mind when I did that, which was dumb and bad."

5 | Solicit information.

Trick your partner into filling you in on what you have done wrong by feigning interest in learning how to do it better next time. "Why don't you tell me exactly what it was that bothered you so much, so I never do it again." Once it is clear what you did, offer an event-specific apology and/or excuse.

6 | Offer a guarantee of universally improved performance in future.

Promise that you will do better in all aspects, in all ways, from now on.

EMERGENCY PHRASES FOR WHEN YOU'RE IN THE DOGHOUSE

- "You look so cute/young/thin when you're mad."

- "I was just thinking, we haven't been to [insert name of partner's favorite restaurant] in ages."

- "You know what I suddenly feel like doing? Vacuuming/ Cooking/Watching the kids while you get your nails done."

- "In the long run, this isn't going to seem like such a big deal."

- "I got you flowers/a necklace/flowers and a diamond necklace."

- "The important thing is that we have each other."

- "What? What? Where am I? I feel so strange . . . like all the events of the last few days were the result of some sort of alien that took control of my mind."

Phrase of Last Resort: "I was wrong."

| *how to apologize when you don't know what you've done wrong*

HOW TO SLEEP ON THE COUCH

1 Remove the back cushions.
If the couch has loose back cushions, take them off to add more width to the sleeping surface.

2 Remove the arm cushions.
Side cushions take up precious head and leg room, and will just end up on the floor in the middle of the night anyway.

3 Fluff and flip.
If the sofa design permits, remove the seat cushions, fluff them, then flip them so the side that was down is now the top. This will provide a more even sleeping surface.

4 Cover the seat cushions with a sheet.
The sheet will protect your face from odors trapped in the cushions and will protect the seating area from saliva.

5 Use your usual pillow.
You will sleep better with your head resting on a familiar pillow. Get yours from the bedroom, if the bedroom is still accessible to you.

6 Depending on the temperature of the room and your comfort level, get a sheet, blanket, comforter, or large towel to put on top of you.

7 Relax.
Do not go to bed angry.

Be Aware
If you are an active sleeper, lay the sofa cushions on the floor next to the sofa to break your fall should you roll off during the night.

USEFUL EXCUSES

This never happened to me before.
I had a really tough day at work.
Not tonight, I have a meeting.
I have to get up early.
I'm too drunk.
I'm not drunk enough.
My turtle died.
I'm gay.
I'm straight.
I can't decide.
It's an old football injury.
I forgot my wallet.
I have to wash my hair.
I am leaving the country.
I need to take my medication.
I couldn't find a place to park.
I couldn't get a cab.
I left it in the cab.
I have to catch a plane.
I buy it for the articles.
They're supposed to test them at the factory.
Nobody's perfect.
I warned you about me.
We don't know each other well enough.
We know each other too well for that.
I didn't think you were coming back today.
He/she needed a friend.
It meant nothing to me.

Someone told me it was an art film.
We might learn some new things from it.
I have a bad back.
I have bad knees.
I asked you first.
I have to walk my dog.
That's not what I meant.
I don't remember saying that.
I'm terrible with names.
I can't bend over that far.
I didn't think you would notice.
My pager is broken.
My cell phone needs recharging.
My computer has a virus.
Your voicemail was full.
Your server must have been down.
I thought you meant next Friday.
It won't stain.
They're family.
I thought you understood without my having
    to say it.
Next time will be better.

ITEMS YOU SHOULD NOT USE AS A PACIFER

bottle

cell phone

lightbulb

Ping-Pong paddle

salt or pepper shaker

screwdriver

toilet plunger handle

HOW TO MAKE AN EMERGENCY BOTTLE

⭐ **Use a medicine dropper or turkey baster.**
Dribble milk (or formula or other liquid) into the side of the baby's mouth. Allow time for swallowing before inserting the next dropperful.

⭐ **Use a straw.**
Suck fluid into a straw and sustain tension by placing your thumb on the top of the straw. Put the straw into the side of the baby's mouth and remove your thumb periodically from the straw, releasing the tension and allowing the liquid to dribble out at intervals.

⭐ **Use a gravy boat.**
Slowly pour small amounts of liquid into the baby's mouth with the spout directing intake. Small creamers from tea sets can also be used. Even better are creamers from children's tea sets.

⭐ **Use a water gun.**
Fill the barrel with milk. Gently pull the trigger and squirt milk into the side of the baby's mouth.

⭐ **Use a sports water bottle.**
Squeeze milk into the baby's mouth.

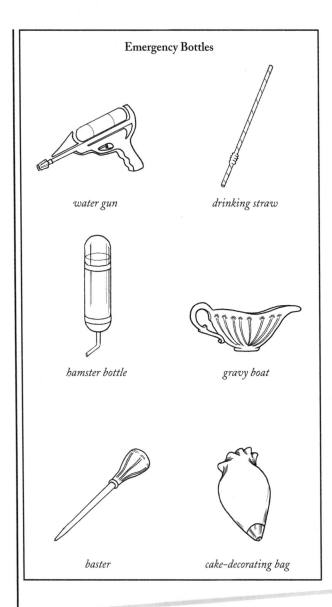

Emergency Bottles

water gun

drinking straw

hamster bottle

gravy boat

baster

cake-decorating bag

Use a cake-decorating bag.

Fill the bag three-quarters full with milk, keeping your finger over the hole of the decorating tip. Twist the end of the bag and hold it closed to contain the milk. Gingerly insert the tip into the baby's mouth at regular intervals and control the flow of the milk with your fingertip. Round, oval, and leaf decorating tips are preferable.

 Use a hamster bottle.

Sterilize the bottle and tube. Fill the bottle with milk. The leakproof vacuum will prevent the milk from spilling. Do not secure the bottle onto a car seat or bassinet for self-feeding.

Be Aware

Do not use airplane mini-bottles or rubber gloves or balloons with a hole poked in the end as substitute bottles.

HOW TO RID A BEDROOM OF MONSTERS

1 Turn on the lights.
Show your child that there are no monsters in the room.

2 Explain that you are making sure there will be no monsters in the future.

3 Spray infested areas with water.
Monsters are afraid of water. Fill a spray bottle with water and lightly mist problem areas, including under the bed, around the door, and in the closet.

4 Place sentries outside of closets and by windows.
Monsters will avoid friendly-looking stuffed animals, dolls, clowns, and puppets. Assemble a battalion of these around all likely points of entry.

5 Use the color green.
Many monsters are afraid of the color green. Use a green night light or encourage your child to wear pajamas with some green on them. A bandage, washable tattoo, nail polish, or a sticker with the color green are also effective.

Be Aware
If you encounter monsters, kill them with kindness.

HOW TO REMOVE A WAD OF PAPER FROM YOUR CHILD'S NOSE

1 Pull gently on any protruding paper.
Pinch the paper firmly between your index finger and thumb. Pull with a steady downward motion until the wad comes free, taking care not to rip it. If the wad does not budge, or if no paper protrudes, continue to the next step.

2 Sterilize a pair of tweezers.
Rub them with hydrogen peroxide or isopropyl alcohol.

3 Tilt the child's head back to give you a clear view of the nostril and tissue wad.
Use a flashlight or desk lamp for better visibility. Hold the child's head steady.

4 Insert the tweezers into the nose.
Place the tip of the tweezers around as much of the paper wad as possible. Make certain the tweezers have a firm grasp on the paper wad or you risk tearing off small pieces and prolonging the job. Do not push the wad deeper into the nostril.

5 Pull steadily.
Do not yank the wad. Have a clean tissue or handkerchief ready to absorb any leakage.

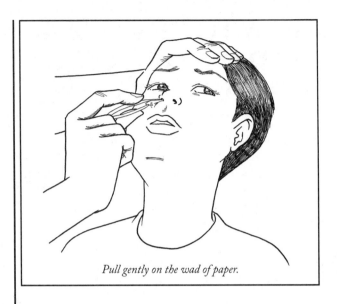

Pull gently on the wad of paper.

6 Discard the wad.
Wash hands thoroughly.

How to Remove a Pea, Marble, or Other Solid Object

1 Place your mouth over the child's mouth.
The position is the same as for mouth-to-mouth resuscitation.

2 Press the unclogged nostril closed with your finger.

3 Blow.
Blow a short but forceful puff into the child's mouth. The stuck object should pop free.

HOW TO DEAL WITH A DEAD PET

1 Make sure the pet is really dead.

Cats often sleep without moving for hours, dogs can be lazy, reptiles are cold blooded and still, fish with parasites sometimes float upside down at the surface, and opossums are well known for feigning. Observe the pet's chest: If it rises and falls, even very slowly, the animal is still alive. Hold a mirror to the pet's nose. If no condensation appears, the animal is probably dead. Pick up the animal. If it does not move and its body is stiff and cold, it has passed away. Feel the neck for a pulse. If you cannot feel one, and all the other signs indicate death, the pet has died. Finally, check for involuntary blinking reflex: Lightly touch the pet's cornea. Any animal that is alive will blink reflexively.

2 Break the news to your child.

If the pet's death was sudden and unexpected, the child is likely to be distraught. Explain that death is a fact of life. Emphasize that the pet had a happy life, the child had taken good care of it, and that the pet is not suffering.

3 Prepare the body.

Close the animal's eyelids—you may need to hold them in place for several seconds so they will stay closed. Place the corpse in a matchbox, shoe box, or wooden box and cover with a washcloth, towel, or sheet, depending on the size of the pet.

4 Hold a family funeral.
Pets are a part of the family, and children expect them to be buried when they die. Give everyone a chance to speak at the funeral ceremony. Burial should immediately follow the ceremony, though there may be laws restricting the burial of pets in a yard. Check with your local vet on burial options, or contact a pet cemetery.

5 Allow your child to grieve.
Do not replace the pet right away. Grieving is an important part of the recovery process, and children should be given time to adapt to the loss.

Be Aware
• A pet cemetery charges from $100 to many thousands of dollars, depending on the coffin, type of service, and size and quality of the headstone/plaque.
• Many vets have cremation services available. If the local vet cannot help with disposal, the local public health department or any large veterinary hospital or university will have facilities.

HOW TO DEAL WITH A SMART ALECK

1 Ignore.
Children with easy-going temperaments will try out smart-aleck behavior once or twice and drop it if it doesn't get a response.

2 Alert your child to the offensive behavior.
If your child continues to display an impertinent attitude, point out specific information about his actions that are unacceptable. Raise a yellow flag, kept in your back pocket (the way a referee calls a foul), whenever your child says something obnoxious. Then give him a time-out.

3 Remove privileges.
Reduce access to favorite activities, such as watching TV or playing outside, in accordance with the severity and frequency of the insolence. Clearly state the reason for the consequence. Place favorite toys or video games in a "toy prison," from which they can be paroled for the child's good behavior.

4 Do not sass back.
It will be tempting to respond in kind to offensive behavior; it is likely that you'd win a contest of wits, but you run the risk of encouraging your child to come up with better lines the next time.

5 Encourage your budding comedian.

Try to hone your child's wit into a marketable skill. Watch movies and listen to recordings featuring famous sarcastic comedians and work on his act. Beware that this could lead to the child becoming a "dirty talker," and, if the act succeeds, completely unmanageable.

Be Aware

Children learn to behave and speak by modeling what they observe at home. Do not use any language in front of the child that you would not want him repeating. Eliminate sarcasm, eye rolling, verbal mimicry, irony, and back talk from your own speech.

HOW TO SURVIVE YOUR CHILD'S FIRST DATE

1 Meditate.

A few hours before the date, exercise, practice yoga or tai chi, or meditate. Take deep breaths in through your nose and out through your mouth. Listen to soothing music. If you take an antianxiety medication, make sure that you do not miss a dose that day. Alternatively, consume one cocktail 30 to 45 minutes before the date is scheduled to begin.

2 Lay the ground rules.

Inform your teen that you have a few simple requirements before she leaves on her date:

- Completion of a "dating plan" before departure, including the name of the date, age, and contact information, the intended venues and activities for the date, the names and contact information for other participants, and approximate time frame.
- Approval of attire, including amount of skin visible, number of tears in clothes, color and style of hair, makeup, and jewelry.
- Date must come inside to pick up her up. Honking or calling via cell phone when outside the house is not acceptable.
- Ask now any questions she has about the "birds and the bees."

*If the date does not meet your gaze and withdraws his hand
quickly, you know you are in control.*

- Curfews must be adhered to.
- Promise to call for any reason, including having a
  bad time, want a ride home, will be late—but can't
  be late.

3 Shake hands with the date.
Greet him with an unnecessarily long, firm handshake and good eye contact. If the date looks away and
attempts to withdraw his hand quickly, this is a positive sign—you are making him uncomfortable; you
are in control. If the date attempts to overpower your
handshake and meets your gaze with a steely glare, he
is challenging you and you should be worried.

4 | Assess the date's attire.
Dressing too provocatively or too conservatively means the date is working too hard on his image.

5 | Assess the date's age.
Excess facial or gray hair, crow's feet, and telltale phrases such as "when I was your age," "back in the day," and "they don't make them like they used to" are signs that your teen's date is no longer a teen himself.

6 | Remind yourself that dating is a rite of passage, that you survived, and that your teen will, too.

GAMES TO PLAY WHILE WAITING UP

★ | Guess the arrival time.
Each parent guesses the exact arrival time of the teen (hour and minute). As the chosen times pass with no arrival, each parent picks a new time. The parent with the time closest to the actual arrival wins.

★ | Pick the excuse.
Each parent chooses three excuses the teen may use upon late arrival. The parent with the right excuse is the winner.

★ | Name the commercial.
Turn on the TV. The first person to correctly pick the name of the product being advertised—before it is mentioned—wins.

Be Aware

- Do not talk too long with the date. Five minutes of polite conversation is adequate when meeting the date. Do not show home movies or flip through photo albums. Do not take the date's picture or attempt to videotape the first date.
- Give your child a watch that is set ten minutes fast.
- Avoid direct interrogation. Do not say, "So, what are your intentions with my daughter?"
- Do not tag along on your child's first date. If you must see what goes on, follow from at least three or four cars back.

DIRECT QUESTION	TACTFUL QUESTION
How old are you?	Who did you vote for in the last election? The one before that?
Do you smoke?	Want a smoke?
Are you an alcoholic?	Want a drink?
Do you do drugs?	Are you holding?
What are your intentions?	Will I be seeing you again?

HOW TO BOND WITH YOUR TEENAGER

PERFORM AN OLLIE ON A SKATEBOARD

1 Position your feet on the board.
Place your nondominant foot toward the front of the deck (the wooden part of the board) over the trucks (front axle). Place the foot at a comfortable angle, not quite forward and not completely to the side. Angle your dominant foot across the board at the tail (rear end) of the board.

2 Bend your knees.
Your knees should be slightly bent to help you keep your balance.

3 Propel the board slowly forward.
Remove your back foot from the deck and use it to push on the ground and propel the board forward. Once it begins rolling, put your foot back in place at the rear of the board.

4 Slide your front foot back.
Move your front foot back about six inches, toward the middle of the deck.

Kick down hard on the tail of the deck.
The front of the board will rise off the ground.

Land.

5 | Kick the tail down.

Kick down hard on the tail section of the deck, while at the same time lifting your front foot up and springing up off your back foot. The front of the board will rise off the ground.

6 | Move your front foot forward.

With the front of the board still in the air, move your front foot forward slightly while airborne. This will raise the tail section and get the skateboard completely off the ground. You may find it easier to simply rotate your front ankle, so the board is pivoting on the outside edge of your leading foot.

7 | Stay centered over the deck.

While floating in midair, keep your feet centered over the board, since you will need to be properly positioned to land. Both you and the skateboard will be traveling forward at the same rate of speed, so this is a natural movement.

8 | Let gravity take the board back.

The board will land with the wheels down, since the wheels and axles are heavier than the deck.

9 | Land on the board.

Bend your knees to help absorb the impact of the landing.

DJ A PARTY

1 Spin the first record.
Select a song with a strong intro to establish the tone for the rest of the set. Place the first record on the left deck (or record player). Move the crossfader all the way to the left, so that channel will play the music. The left deck corresponds with channel one, the right deck corresponds with channel two.

2 Drop the needle.
Put the needle down on your record to play the song for the crowd.

3 Plug in the headphones.
The mixer has a cue input, or a ¼-inch jack for headphones, that allows you to hear what's coming up next without broadcasting the music over the speakers.

4 Cue up a song.
Select the next track to blend with the song that is now playing through the speakers. Put the new track on the right deck, which will play on channel two, and make sure that the cue is set to play channel two. Hold one headphone to your ear, leaving your other ear free to hear the music playing to the house and to gauge the crowd reaction.

5 Line up eight counts.
Count from one to eight in time with the beats (or bass drum hits) of the song playing over the speaker.

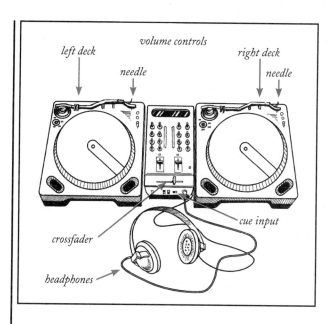

volume controls

left deck

needle

right deck

needle

cue input

crossfader

headphones

Play the cue song over your headphones, and line up the eight counts so the "1s" match. Use your finger to slow down or start the record on channel two to match the beats.

6 Cross fade into the new track.
The crossfader is a rectangular slider control located at the bottom of the mixer. It slides horizontally rather than vertically, like the volume controls. Use the crossfader to blend the two channels.

7 Maintain song continuity.
Mixing the two songs at the right place is critical to keeping the crowd involved and dancing. Most dance

songs and DJ remixes have breaks, or areas of the song where the vocals and music purposely drop out and give you a chance to beat mix. Avoid mixing into or out of a track during a vocal segment.

8 | Watch the crowd.

The crowd is the best gauge of how well you are DJing. If people are having fun—and, especially, if they are easily dancing through the transitions between songs— you are doing a good job. If, on the other hand, they are having trouble dancing to the beat, alter your song selections.

Be Aware

- Every mixer is different. Familiarize yourself with the equipment in the booth.

- Using a stopwatch or a watch or clock with a second hand, count the beats of the current song (or bass drum hits) for 15 seconds, then multiply by four to determine the number of beats per minute (BPM). Most sets begin with songs with a lower BPM, then gradually increase the BPM as the music increases in intensity. As a general rule, consider 88 to 110 BPM for a hip hop or rap music set, and 116 to 140 BPM for a house/techno set.

- Do not play the new song at a lower volume after the fade in. The volumes of the two songs should match, since a lower volume diminishes a song's energy.

ESSENTIAL PARENTAL CLICHÉS

When I was your age, we . . .
Because you're the child and I'm the parent.
Life isn't fair.
When you're the parent, you'll make the rules.
They call it bedtime for a reason.
Do I have to come up/in/over there?
You're bored? I'm Dad, nice to meet you.
Just a few more minutes/miles.
Don't make me tell you again.
That's twice. Three strikes and you're out.
You make a better door than a window.
Eat your vegetables.
So, I guess you don't like dessert anymore?
Because it's my house.
Because it's my car.
Because I'm the parent.
Just because.
There's no allowance without "allow."
I can't wait until you have kids.
Can you keep the noise down to a dull roar?
Are you trying to heat/cool the entire
    neighborhood?
Money doesn't grow on trees.
I'll give you something to cry about.
Maybe.
You'll spoil your dinner.
Find something to do.

293. *essential parental cliches*

Do you have something you want to tell me about?

You won't be happy until someone loses an eye.

If [fill in blank] jumped off a bridge, would you?

I hope your kids are just like you.

When I was your age, we didn't have . . .

This is why we can't have nice things.

You're not going out looking like that.

No son/daughter of mine is . . .

This is going to hurt me more than it hurts you.

Do you want to catch pneumonia?

I do and do and do for you kids and this is the thanks I get.

This is why I have gray hair.

You have nothing to do? I'll give you something to do.

There are children starving in . . .

Because it's good for you.

Don't make me ask you again.

The food left on your plate could feed a small village in . . .

Your face is going to stay like that.

Too bad, so sad.

Go to your room to cry.

Because I said so.

While you're under my roof, you follow my rules.

Children should be seen and not heard.

Don't make me pull this car over.

Go ask your mother.

HOW TO BREAK UP
A CAT FIGHT

1 Identify the aggressor.
Look for the cat that is on top of the other one. This is the aggressor.

2 Scold the aggressor.
In a loud voice, yell "NO," "STOP," or "THAT'S ENOUGH!" and the aggressor's name.

3 Make loud noises.
Clap your hands, stomp your feet, or bang two pot lids together.

4 Physically separate the cats.
Use a long-handled implement such as a mop or broom, to nudge the cats apart. If the fight is happening outside, throw water or turn a hose onto them.

5 "Scruff" the aggressor cat.
Grasp the aggressor cat by the loose skin at the back of his neck. Remove him from the other cat and push him toward the floor with firm but gentle pressure. Hiss loudly. While the aggressor is being scruffed, allow the victim cat to flee the area.

6 Keep the cats apart.
Separate the aggressor and victim cat for one hour. If aggressive behavior resumes, establish a "safe room"

Use a long-handled broom to nudge the cats apart.
Throw water or turn a hose on them.

for the aggressor and reintroduce the cats to each other over a week-long period.

Be Aware

- Do not get in the middle of a cat fight and try to pry the cats apart physically. The cats will instinctively treat you as another combatant.
- Play fighting is a part of a healthy cat's social life and needn't be discouraged. If the cats are frequently switching roles (one chasing, the other being chased; one pouncing, the other acting as "prey") and neither cat is hissing or showing teeth, do not intervene.

HOW TO TOILET TRAIN YOUR CAT

1 Move the litter box next to the toilet.

2 Incrementally raise the litter box to the level
of the toilet.
Place telephone books or encyclopedias under the
litter box, one at a time, until the box is at the same
height level as the toilet. Wait each time until your cat
is adjusted and comfortable with the new level before
raising the level again.

3 Leave the litter box in this raised, toilet-adjacent
position.
The box should be positioned so that the cat must step
across the toilet to access her litter box. Leave it there
until your cat is accustomed to the feel of walking on
the toilet seat.

4 Move the litter box on top of the toilet seat.
Leave it in this position for several days, so your cat
becomes used to doing her business on top of the toilet. When you use the toilet, remove the litter box and
then replace it when you're done.

5 Remove the litter box from the top of the toilet seat.

6 Place a mixing bowl in the toilet.

Select a bowl that fits snugly in the toilet bowl. Fill it with two to three inches of cat litter. Humans using the toilet should first remove the metal mixing bowl.

7 Position the cat's feet.

Watch your cat constantly over a period of several days. Every time she goes to the toilet to urinate or defecate, help her set her feet correctly on the lid of the toilet: Two paws on the front and two paws in the rear, so she is squatting over the mixing bowl.

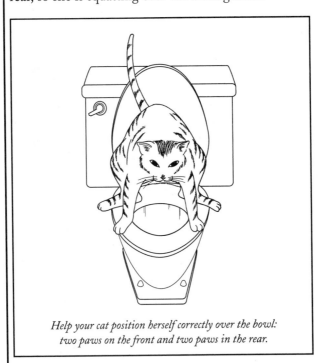

*Help your cat position herself correctly over the bowl:
two paws on the front and two paws in the rear.*

8 Replace the cat litter in the mixing bowl with water.
Continue helping your cat position herself correctly
over the bowl, and encourage her, so she becomes
used to the sound of doing her business into water.
Each time your cat relieves herself successfully in the
mixing bowl, empty it into the toilet and flush it while
she watches.

9 Remove the mixing bowl from the toilet.
Once your cat has become used to relieving
herself into water while sitting on the toilet, take the
mixing bowl away.

Be Aware

• Once your cat is toilet-trained, the door to the
  bathroom and the toilet lid need to be left open, so
  the cat enjoys free access to the toilet.

• While you may be able to teach a cat to use the
  toilet, it is not generally possible to teach a cat to
  sit, stay, fetch, roll over, speak, shake, come, go, get
  the newspaper, pull a sled, rescue you in the snow,
  or lead you if you are blind.

How to Build a Cat Fort

Cut empty cardboard boxes to expose corrugation and stack with other boxes and carpet remnants to make a cat fort. Rub portions of the fort with catnip to increase interest.

HOW TO TEACH AN OLD DOG NEW TRICKS

⭐ **Be patient.**
You are asking a dog not just to learn something new, but to unlearn her previous way of doing things. This takes time.

⭐ **Credit the dog.**
Convince the dog that she came up with the new trick on her own. If teaching an older canine to "sit," do not try to force her into a sitting position. Instead, praise and reward her when she sits on her own, all the while repeating the "sit" command. Eventually the dog will perform the appropriate behavior when she hears the appropriate word.

⭐ **Keep training sessions short.**
Older dogs tire more easily, so spend only about 10 to 15 minutes on any one training session. Do one in the morning and one in the afternoon, always at the same times.

⭐ **Keep sessions fun.**
Many older, savvy canines "play dumb" during training sessions in order to get out of learning something new.

Consider joining a class. The example of other dogs
may help her catch on.

 Reinforce good behavior.
Use praise and treats to strongly reward compliance.

Be Aware
- Do not go overboard on food rewards. An older, less-active dog may start to put on weight.
- If your dog is particularly stubborn, consider joining a training class. The example of other dogs may help her catch on.

How to Brush Your Dog's Teeth

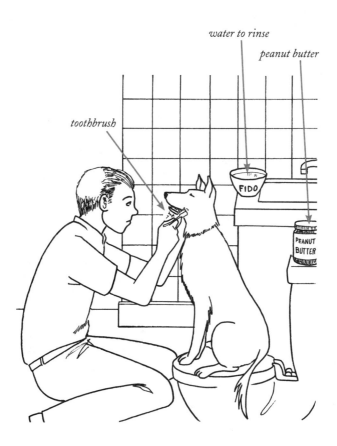

water to rinse

peanut butter

toothbrush

Use peanut butter as toothpaste.

HOW TO OPEN A BOTTLE OF WINE WITH A BROKEN CORK

1 | Examine the cork.
If the cork has broken due to improper corkscrew use, treat the broken cork as if it were whole. If the cork is pushed too far into the bottle, push it all the way in using any long thin implement and proceed to "With a Very Dry Cork," step 5, below.

2 | Reinsert the corkscrew.
Six half turns of the corkscrew will usually be enough to allow you to remove a full cork, but you may need fewer for a partial cork. Turn the corkscrew slowly to prevent further cork breakage.

3 | Pull the cork out.
Pull up steadily on the corkscrew, being careful not to jerk the cork out of the bottle. If the cork remains in the bottle, go to "With a Very Dry Cork," step 2, below.

WITH A VERY DRY CORK

1 | Check for crumbling.
If the cork is soft and powdery, it will not offer the corkscrew enough resistance. It may also be stuck to

the sides of the bottle, making intact removal impossible. Bore a hole through the center of the cork. Use the corkscrew as a drill.

2 | Widen the hole.
Wiggle the corkscrew from side to side to increase the diameter of the hole.

3 | Try to pour.
If the wine will not pour, continue to enlarge the diameter of the hole as above, or force the remainder of the cork into the bottle (see "How to Open a Bottle of Wine Without a Corkscrew," page 306).

4 | Make a filter.
Place a piece of clean, unwaxed, unbleached cheesecloth over the mouth of a decanter and secure it tightly with a rubber band. If no cheesecloth is available, use a coffee filter (preferably unbleached). Do not use a T-shirt or any article of clothing you have washed in detergent—the detergent can affect the taste of the wine.

5 | Strain the wine.
Carefully pour the wine through the filter into the decanter. When the bottle is empty, remove the filter containing the pieces of cork from the mouth of the decanter and serve the wine.

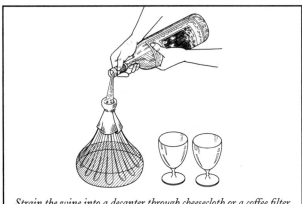

Strain the wine into a decanter through cheesecloth or a coffee filter.

HOW TO OPEN A BOTTLE OF WINE WITHOUT A CORKSCREW

It is virtually impossible to remove a cork from a wine bottle without a device made for this purpose. However, the cork can be pushed into the bottle with a little effort.

1 Hold the bottle steady with one hand.

2 Use a blunt, unbreakable, skinny object, such as a screwdriver, the handle of a wooden mixing spoon, or a butter knife to push the cork in.

3 Apply steady pressure and be patient.
You may carefully tap the end of the blunt object with a hammer or meat tenderizer to force the cork into the bottle more quickly.

HOW TO AVOID SHOOTING A CHAMPAGNE CORK

1 Hold the thumb of your nondominant hand over the cage and cork.

The cork may fly out of the bottle as soon as the wire mesh (known as the "cage") is loosened. Keep pressure on the cork and point the bottle away from yourself and anyone nearby.

2 Turn the key of the wire cage.

All cages on champagne and sparkling wine open after six clockwise half-turns. Remove the cage.

3 Place an opened cloth napkin over the cork and neck of the bottle.

Hold the bottle in your nondominant hand and the napkin over the cork in your other hand. Keep the bottle angled away from people.

4 Hold the cork tightly and slowly turn the bottle clockwise.

Do not turn the cork or you risk breaking it.

5 As the cork begins to come out, apply downward pressure on it.

The pressure will prevent the cork from shooting away from the bottle.

Turn the key of the wire cage six clockwise half-turns while keeping constant pressure on the cage and cork.

Cover the cork and neck of the bottle with a cloth napkin. Carefully turn the bottle clockwise until the cork pops.

6 | Hold the cork at the mouth of the bottle for five seconds.
If champagne begins to bubble up and out, it will react with the end of the cork and flow back into the bottle.

7 | Slowly pour the champagne.
Pour the champagne slowly until the froth (called "mousse") reaches about ⅔ up the glass, then pause. When the mousse has receded, continue filling until the glass is approximately ⅔ full.

Be Aware

- The quieter the pop, the better the opening. A poor opening will cause champagne to spurt out of the bottle, resulting in lost champagne and carbonation.
- An uncontrolled opening may result in the cork leaving the champagne bottle with enough force to cause injury to someone nearby.
- Crystal flutes will improve the champagne experience: The slender shape makes the long streams of bubbles more visually appealing and concentrates the aroma. The finest leaded crystal (with a lead content of about 25 percent) has the smoothest surface and allows the champagne to maintain maximum carbonation.
- Never chill champagne flutes.
- Avoid champagne "saucers": Their larger surface area releases more carbonation.
- The smaller the bubbles, the better the champagne.

Never uncork a champagne bottle while facing a crowd.

BEER TO FOOD EQUIVALENCY CHART

Food item	Calorie equivalent in mugs of beer*
Apple pie, 1 slice	🍺🍺🍺🍺
Bagel with cream cheese	🍺🍺
Beef jerky, 1 stick	🍺
Breadsticks with marinara sauce, 6	🍺🍺🍺
Brownie, frosted	🍺
Burrito, bean and cheese	🍺🍺🍺
Cheeseburger	🍺🍺🍺🍺
Chicken breast, fried	🍺🍺🍺
Chicken fingers, 6	🍺🍺🍺
Chili, 1 cup	🍺🍺
Chocolate chip cookies, 10	🍺🍺🍺🍺🍺
Coffee with 2 tbsp. cream	🍺
Cola, 12-oz can	🍺
Dip, French onion, ¼ cup	🍺
Double bacon cheeseburger	🍺🍺🍺🍺
Doughnut, glazed	🍺🍺
Eggs Benedict	🍺🍺🍺🍺🍺
Falafel in pita with yogurt dressing	🍺🍺🍺🍺
French fries, medium size	🍺🍺🍺
Fried-egg bagel sandwich, bacon and cheese	🍺🍺🍺🍺
Fried rice, vegetarian	🍺🍺🍺
Frozen yogurt, chocolate, ½ cup	🍺
Hot fudge sundae, small	🍺
Hot wings, 8	🍺🍺🍺🍺
Hummus and pita bread	🍺🍺🍺
Latte, low-fat	🍺
Macaroni and cheese, 1 cup	🍺🍺

Milkshake, chocolate, 10 oz.......................................

Muffin, blueberry, large..

Nachos, 8 ....

Pad Thai with chicken and shrimp ....

Pho ....

Pizza, pepperoni slice ....

Popcorn, microwave popped, ½ bag......................

Potato, baked, plain ....

Potato chips, 6-oz bag ....

Ramen noodles, 1 package....................................

Salad dressing, balsamic vinaigrette, ¼ cup...........

Salad dressing, ranch, ¼ cup................................

Sandwich, corned beef on rye ....

Sandwich, peanut butter and jelly........................

Sesame chicken ....

Spaghetti with meatballs ....

Sugary breakfast cereal, 1 bowl, no milk ....

Taco, beef..

Cocktails

Beer, light, mug...

Bloody Mary ....

Cosmopolitan..

Daiquiri ....

Fuzzy navel ....

Gin and tonic ....

Grain alcohol, shot...

Kamikaze ....

Long Island iced tea...

Malt liquor, 40 oz..

Margarita ....

Martini .... 🍺

Mudslide.. 🍺 🍺 🍺

Piña Colada .... 🍺 🍺

Rum, shot .... 🍺

Rum and Coke... 🍺

Screwdriver .... 🍺 🍺

Seabreeze .... 🍺

Sex on the beach .... 🍺 🍺

Tequila, shot.. 🍺

Vodka, shot .... 🍺

Whiskey, shot... 🍺

Whiskey sour .... 🍺

Wine, glass... 🍺

Wine cooler .... 🍺 🍺

* One mug of beer is equivalent to 150 calories.

beer to food equivalency chart

ESSENTIAL MANLY DRINK RECIPES

⭐ BRAVE BULL

2 ounces tequila
1 ounce Kahlúa
Lime wedge

Shake the tequila and Kahlúa with ice, then strain into an old-fashioned glass with ice. Garnish with the lime.

⭐ CORDLESS SCREWDRIVER

2 ounces vodka, chilled
Orange wedge, coated in superfine sugar

Pour the chilled vodka into a shot glass. Drink the vodka, then bite into an orange wedge coated with superfine sugar.

⭐ HORNY LEPRECHAUN

¾ ounce Bailey's Irish Cream
¾ ounce Rumple Minze
2 dashes heavy cream

Shake all ingredients with ice, then strain into a chilled cordial glass.

✪ | Horse's Neck

1 horse's neck orange peel spiral
2 ounces bourbon
4 ounces chilled ginger ale

Drape the spiral around three or four ice cubes in a highball glass, and hang the end of the peel over the edge of the glass. This is the "horse's neck." Add the bourbon and ginger ale.

✪ | Godfather

2 ounces Scotch
1 ounce amaretto

Pour both ingredients over ice in an old-fashioned glass, and stir.

✪ | Prairie Oyster

1 egg
1 ounce vodka
2 dashes vinegar
1 teaspoon Worcestershire sauce
1 teaspoon ketchup
2 dashes Tabasco sauce
Pinch of salt and pepper

essential manly drink recipes

Crack the egg into an old-fashioned glass, taking care not to break the yolk. Add the remaining ingredients. Drink in a single gulp.

⭐ RUSTY NAIL

2 ounces Scotch
1 ounce Drambuie

Pour both ingredients over ice in a heavy old-fashioned glass, and stir.

⭐ SATAN'S WHISKERS

1 ounce gin
1 ounce fresh orange juice
½ ounce dry vermouth
½ ounce sweet vermouth
½ ounce Grand Marnier
Dash of bitters
Orange peel twist

Shake the gin, orange juice, dry and sweet vermouths, Grand Marnier, and bitters with ice, then strain into a chilled cocktail glass. Garnish with the orange peel.

⭐ SUFFERING BASTARD

1 ounce light rum
1 ounce dark rum
1 ounce Cointreau or triple sec

1 teaspoon orgeat
1 ounce fresh lime juice
2 ounces fresh orange juice
Tropical fruit, such as pineapple, kiwi, or citrus

Shake both rums, Cointreau, orgeat, lime juice, and orange juice with ice, then strain into a chilled hurricane glass filled with ice. Garnish with fruit.

HANGOVER REMEDIES

- A pint of beer and a bowl of salty ceviche

- A bacon, egg, and cheese sandwich, with a cola drink

- A plate of burnt toast

- Two liters of Pedialyte or Gatorade

- Ginger

- Bloody Mary

- Two liters of coconut water

- A quick-absorbing painkiller dissolved in carbonated water

- Orange juice

- Black coffee

- Banana

- Applesauce

essential manly drink recipes

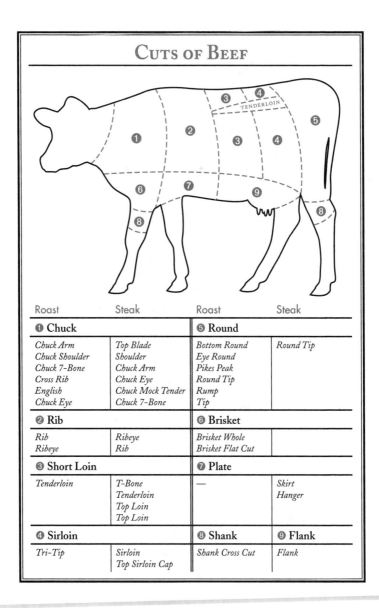

Cuts of Beef

Roast	Steak	Roast	Steak
❶ Chuck		**❺ Round**	
Chuck Arm	Top Blade	Bottom Round	Round Tip
Chuck Shoulder	Shoulder	Eye Round	
Chuck 7-Bone	Chuck Arm	Pikes Peak	
Cross Rib	Chuck Eye	Round Tip	
English	Chuck Mock Tender	Rump	
Chuck Eye	Chuck 7-Bone	Tip	
❷ Rib		**❻ Brisket**	
Rib	Ribeye	Brisket Whole	
Ribeye	Rib	Brisket Flat Cut	
❸ Short Loin		**❼ Plate**	
Tenderloin	T-Bone	—	Skirt
	Tenderloin		Hanger
	Top Loin		
	Top Loin		
❹ Sirloin		**❽ Shank**	**❾ Flank**
Tri-Tip	Sirloin	Shank Cross Cut	Flank
	Top Sirloin Cap		

CUTS OF PORK

Roast	Other Cuts	Roast	Other Cuts
❶ Boston-Style Shoulder		**❹ Side**	
Pork Shoulder *Boston Butt*	*Boston Butt Steaks* *Pork Shoulder Butt* *Ground Pork*	—	*Spareribs* *Bacon* *Pork Belly* *Pork Shoulder Hocks* *Pork Leg Hocks*
❷ Arm Picnic Shoulder		**❺ Leg**	
Shoulder Roast	*Smoked Hocks* *Shanks*	*Cured Ham* *Fresh Leg*	*Pork Leg* *Pork Steak*
❸ Loin			
Loin Rib Roast	*Pork Tenderloin* *Loin Chops* *Pork Loin* *Back* *Pork Chops* *Country-style Ribs*		

MEAT GRILLING TIPS

⭐ Brush steak with a small coating of olive oil and rub with kosher salt to seal in flavor.

⭐ Never trim the fat from steak; if trimming is insisted upon by non-man members of the party, only trim after the steak is grilled.

⭐ Let your grill "hot up" for 10 minutes before applying meat.

⭐ Chicken, poultry, and steak all have varying cooking times; establish a "hot zone" and a "medium zone" on your grill to cook things for different times.

⭐ Flip burgers once, and only once, during cooking.

⭐ Flip meat with a spatula, not a fork, to reduce the risk of puncture and subsequent flavor loss.

⭐ Test grilled food with a meat thermometer at the thickest part of the meat. Take meat off the grill just before it reaches the desired temperature, as meat will continue cooking for a few minutes off the heat.

⭐ Do not, under any circumstances, grill vegetable skewers.

How to Rescue Fish
That is Flaking Apart

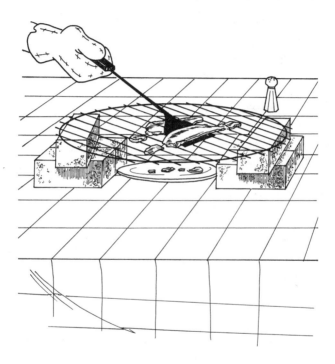

Remove the metal grill from the flame using barbecue mitts.
Place the grill between two stacks of two bricks, with the fish over
an open center area. Place a pan under the grill/fish to catch flaking
pieces, then remove remaining fish with a spatula coated in olive oil
or butter. Garnish with lemon and serve as fish hash.

HOW TO PUT OUT A GRILL FIRE

1 If you can safely reach the knobs, turn off the burners on a gas or propane grill.

If a propane tank itself is involved in the fire, evacuate the vicinity and call emergency services immediately.

2 Smother the fire.

Never spray water onto a grease fire. It will intensify the flames and spread the burning grease to a wider area. Throw salt, baking soda, or sand onto the fire to smother the flames.

3 Close the lid.

Make sure all grill vents are closed to further starve the fire of oxygen.

4 If the fire is still burning after 30 seconds, douse the grill with a fire extinguisher.

Be Aware

Flare-ups are usually caused by excess fat and grease dripping from meat through the grates. To prevent a flare-up from getting out of control, quickly move food to a warming rack with a pair of long-handled tongs. Return each piece to the center of the grill one by one, let the excess fat burn off, and remove it to the warming rack again. When every piece has been treated in this fashion, return all the food to the grill and continue cooking.

How to Extinguish Burning Clothing

1 Stop moving.
Do not run or flail your limbs, as you will fan the fire, drawing in air and causing flames to burn hotter and more quickly. Running will also cause you to inhale smoke and harmful gasses, and you may spread the fire to other parts of your body, casual onlookers, or nearby objects.

2 Smother the fire.
If you have a fire blanket (or other heavy wool blanket) or bulky covering nearby, wrap it around yourself, patting at the flames. You may succeed in completely smothering the fire. If not, proceed to step 3.

3 Cover your face with your hands.

4 Drop to the ground.
Lie facedown to protect your head from the flames.

5 Roll over repeatedly.
Continue rolling, back and forth or all the way around, as necessary to extinguish all flames.

6 Treat burn areas with cool water.
Apply liberally. Do not break blisters or disturb charred skin. Wrap burn area loosely in dry, sterile bandages. Do not apply creams or ointments.

7 Call emergency services.
For the best chance of recovering all body function and preventing infection, seek professional medical treatment.

Be Aware
Dense fabrics burn more slowly than light, loosely woven garments. If you are barbecuing, wear heavy, tightly knit clothing, such as denim pants or canvas. All-natural fibers (wool, cotton) are best since they tend to burn slowly. Synthetic fibers can be extremely hazardous when aflame, as they will quickly melt, adhering to skin and causing severe burns. Never spray fire-retardants on clothing.

How to Extinguish a Lawn Fire

1 Locate fire-suppression tools.
Instruct others nearby to quickly gather a bucket of water, shovel, and rake.

2 Smother the flames.
Apply water liberally or, if none is available, use a shovel to dig soil or sand and cover the fire. A long-handled shovel with a wide blade can be used to

Douse the flames with any available water
or nonflammable beverages.

how to put out a grill fire

swat or tamp out errant flames. Stand well back from blazing grass as you attempt to put out the fire.

3 | Clear the area of fuel.
As you dig or tamp, push flammable items, such as leaves or brush, away from the path of the fire.

4 | If you are unable to extinguish the fire, use the rake or shovel to clear a path to safety.

5 | Call emergency services.

Grilling Safety

- **Grill on level ground at least 10 feet from buildings, trees, or brush.** Do not grill on a balcony, terrace, roof, or any structure that can catch fire.

- **Wear safe clothing.** Avoid untucked shirt tails, loose sleeves, and aprons with long strings. Use flame-retardant grilling mitts to protect hands and arms.

- **Never leave a grill unattended once it's lit.**

Charcoal Grills

- **Never use a charcoal or gas grill in an enclosed area.** Even with a window open or a fan ventilating the area, carbon monoxide produced by burning charcoal or gas can collect indoors and kill you. Carbon monoxide has no odor or color, so you will not be aware of its presence.

- **Do not add starter fluid to an existing fire.** The flame may attach to the liquid as you squirt it on, forming an arc of fire back to the bottle in your hands.

Gas Grills

- **Open the lid before lighting a propane grill.** Gas can accumulate inside the grill and explode upon ignition.

- **Check for gas leaks.** At least once a season and every time you replace the gas tank, mix 2 tablespoons of dishwashing detergent with 2 tablespoons of water, open the gas valve, and brush the solution onto all valve connections, tubing connections, and the welds on the tank. Look for growing bubbles at each location. If you find a leak, shut the valve or remove the gas tank and refrain from using the grill until it has been repaired. Do not light the burners while performing a leak test.

CHAPTER 5
WORK

HOW TO SURVIVE
THE INTERVIEW

If You Are Late

1 Call ahead.

If you are stuck in traffic or otherwise running late, call as soon as you know you will be substantially late. Ask to reschedule, either later in the day or on another day.

2 Clean yourself up.

Use a bathroom before meeting your interviewer if you are sweaty and disheveled when you arrive. Wash your face with cold water and blot it dry with paper towels. Gargle. Check your teeth for pieces of food.

3 Apologize.

Tell the interviewer you are sorry for your tardiness, but do not overdo the apology. Do not fabricate an explanation that can easily be verified. The following are acceptable excuses, if true.

• The traffic was terrible.

• There was an accident on the bridge.

• My car caught on fire.

• I was stuck in the elevator.

• I had to take my mother/daughter/pet to the emergency room.

Do not say:
- My alarm clock is broken.
- I lost track of the time.
- I couldn't find my belt.
- I was out so late last night . . .

IF YOU ARE ASKED A DIFFICULT OR LEADING QUESTION

⭐ Always respond with a positive.
If the interviewer says, "I see you don't have experience," counter with, "That's true, but I've always wanted to learn and I'm a quick study!"

⭐ Use personal experiences to demonstrate strengths in areas that are professionally weak.
If the interviewer asks about project management experience and you don't have any, talk about planning your wedding or organizing a large family function (hiring vendors, designing a database, and creating seating charts based on the interests of guests).

⭐ Answer confidently.
It isn't always what you say, but how you say it. Often, questions are designed to assess your professional attitude and maturity level more than your knowledge base. Be sincere in your responses, and act professionally—even if you don't have a good answer. Be straightforward, even when your answer is "I don't know."

✪ Memorize the following good answers to these standard hard-to-address questions:

Q: Where do you see yourself in five years?

A: At a good job in this industry, at a good company, learning and contributing to the company's growth.

Q: Why should I hire you?

A: I've got the right experience, I understand your needs, and I'm a good team player—both in the office and on the softball field.

Q: Why did you quit your last job?

A: I simply wasn't able to contribute to the company's future in the way I wanted. I'm looking for more opportunities for myself, and for a company that can fully utilize my abilities.

✪ Prepare a last-resort response.

If you are asked the one question you dreaded, take a page from the politicians' playbook: Acknowledge the question, then move on. Say, "I'm very glad you asked that, and I'd like to give it some thought. But I'd really like to discuss . . ."

Be Aware

- Always remember the three C's: Cool, Calm, and Confident. An interview is as much about you wanting the job as it is about the job wanting you.
- Always remember the three A's: Ask a lot of questions, Appear clean-cut and well-dressed, and Act to impress.
- Avoid scheduling interviews just after lunch, when most people get sleepy and irritable.

How to Know If You Are Tanking

1 Watch the interviewer's eyes.

An interviewer that is simply going through the motions will not make eye contact. Check for a glazed or glassy stare and heavy or droopy eyelids.

2 Listen carefully.

A bored or disinterested interviewer may quietly hum a tune, whistle softly, or shuffle papers repeatedly.

3 Observe the interviewer's actions.

An interviewer who is constantly checking the time, eating a sandwich, or takes lots of phone calls probably won't offer you the job.

staring at computer

talking on phone

eating sandwich

Watch for signs of a disinterested interviewer.

4 | Pay attention to the amount of time your interviewer speaks versus the amount of time you speak.

If your interviewer speaks more than you do, you may not be coming across very strongly. (On the other hand, some less-experienced interviewers love to hear themselves talk, and may come away with the impression that the interview was very interesting.)

5 | Attempt to rescue the situation.

Your goal at this point should simply be to make it through this interview to the next phase of interviewing, where you can hopefully make a stronger impression. Pick one or more of the following statements designed to get you back in front of the interviewer for a second shot:

- "I'm so certain I'm the right person for this job, I'd be willing to bet my first month's paycheck I'll be your top candidate after round two."

- "The insider knowledge I gained at [insert name of major competitor here] definitely gives me an edge over any other prospective hire. I look forward to talking again soon."

- "The work I did for the CIA/FBI/NSA makes me the perfect choice for this position. I'd love to tell you more about it at a second interview, provided that you have the necessary clearance."

Be Aware

No matter how well the rest of the interview seems to go, you may not be offered the job if any of the following mishaps occur:

- You ask if a photo on your interviewer's desk is his daughter, and it turns out to be his wife.
- You ask to go to the bathroom three times or more, or one trip lasts more than 15 minutes.
- You don't take off your headset during the interview.
- You receive and respond to more than two cell phone calls.
- You make a cell phone call.
- You answer, "A beer would be nice," when your interviewer asks if you'd like something to drink.

HOW TO FLATTER
AN INSECURE BOSS

⭐ Sit next to your boss.

⭐ Loudly agree with your boss's statements.
Enthusiastically say "yes" to each of her suggestions and ideas. Vary your expressions of agreement to include: "I agree," "I totally agree," "I completely agree," and "I couldn't agree more." After your boss completes a declarative statement, add the word "obviously."

⭐ Silently affirm your boss's statements.
Constantly nod as your boss speaks. Smile and chuckle quietly to yourself to express how much you completely agree with what is being said.

⭐ Write down everything your boss says.

⭐ Duplicate your boss's food order.
When someone is taking sandwich orders, wait until after your boss has made her order, and then say "ditto," "the same," or "sounds good."

⭐ Laugh at your boss's jokes.
Watch your boss's body language for signs that what she is saying is meant to be humorous, such as raised eyebrows and teeth showing. Only laugh if you are sure what your boss is saying is meant to be a joke.

Laugh at your boss's jokes.

337. *how to flatter an insecure boss*

★ Take your boss's side in arguments.
When other people continue to disagree with her, roll your eyes and shush them.

★ Ask your boss for advice.
During breaks in the meeting, ask her for counsel on work issues. Write down each piece of advice and thank her profusely. During subsequent conversations, ask for advice on nonwork issues, such as romance, fashion, and family relationships.

★ Offhandedly compliment your boss as you exit the meeting.
As the meeting breaks up, position yourself near the doorway as your boss passes by. Remark to a coworker how enlightening/exciting you found the meeting to be. Place your compliments within a larger pattern. Make such statements such as: "Wow! Another great meeting from [boss's name]."

HOW TO FAKE YOUR WAY THROUGH A PRESENTATION

1 | Speak clearly.
Do not mumble or raise your voice. Speak slowly and evenly. Act as if you are overexplaining very difficult material that the audience might not understand.

2 | Stand up straight.
Project confidence with your body language. Smile and make frequent eye contact with your listeners.

3 | Make up statistics.
Pepper your presentation with facts and figures. Bombard the listeners with numbers. Glance down at notes in your hand so it appears that you are being careful to get the statistics right.

4 | Scrawl.
Use a messy scrawl when writing statistics or other imaginary information on an easel or dry-erase board. Erase each number or flip the page immediately to make room for new fictional information.

5 | Ask the audience questions.
Broad questions such as, "What are the results we're looking for here?" or "Who are our competitors?" or "What are the greatest risks?" will provoke numerous

Make up statistics. Use entertaining props.

and varied responses. Use your presentation time to write them on the board or flip chart.

6 Use entertaining props.
Make a puppet out of a coworker's tie. Pour water from a pitcher into a glass to illustrate how capital flows into the market. Remove your blazer and wave it in front of you as if you are a toreador, taking on the bull-like challenges of a changing economy.

7 Give nonanswers to all questions.
Praise the questioner ("That's a really good question. Thank you for asking that."), insult the questioner ("I don't think we need to waste time explaining that."), or say you'd like to answer but want to keep going ("That falls outside the scope of this presentation.").

8 Conclude with a personal anecdote.
Change the subject from business to a story your father used to tell you. When finished, smile and raise your eyebrows enigmatically.

9 Exit the room.
Say thank you and leave immediately.

THINGS NEVER TO SAY IN A MEETING

Instead of Saying	Say
"I disagree."	"It definitely has possibilities."
"No."	"That's an interesting idea."
"That's the worst idea I've ever heard."	"Let me get back to you on that."
"Let's solve this problem right now."	"Let's schedule a follow-up meeting to discuss potential solutions."
"I will handle it."	"Let's schedule a follow-up meeting to figure out who is going to handle it."
"I'm really attracted to you."	"Let's schedule a follow-up meeting to discuss strategies for implementation."
"I am so bored right now I feel like I'm going to die."	"I have another meeting to get to."
"I am really drunk right now."	Say nothing

HOW TO ESCAPE FROM A MEETING ROOM

⭐ **Create a distraction.**
Use a handheld device with Internet access to order a large food delivery, balloon bouquet, or stripper-gram to the conference room. When the delivery or performer arrives, slip out in the confusion.

⭐ **Go check on something at your desk.**
When asked for a piece of information, explain that the answer is at your desk; get up to fetch it and never return. If asked later, say that while you were away a call came in that you had to take.

⭐ **Fake a telephone call.**
Use an automated application to cause your own phone to ring midmeeting. Look at the incoming call number with an expression of urgent concern and stand up. Mouth "I'm so sorry" to the other attendees as you hurry from the room.

⭐ **Set off the carbon monoxide alarm.**
Nonchalantly lean way back in your seat and press the "test" button on the carbon monoxide alarm, causing the shrill, piercing alarm to go off.

⭐ Become too aggravated to continue.
When someone makes a disagreeable suggestion or presents bad news, throw your arms up, shake your head in exaggerated frustration, and leave the room. Do not use this technique at more than two meetings in a row.

ESCAPE ON A CATERING CART

1 Wait until the food has been brought in and unloaded.

2 Linger at the catering cart.
Sip a cup of coffee. Look casual.

3 Wait until the attendees have returned to their tables and the meeting has resumed.

4 Crouch on the ground.
Tip your plate over so your food spills onto the carpet. Bend over to pick it up and remain on the ground.

5 Climb onto the cart.
Spread aside the tablecloth covering the bottom of the cart. Climb fully inside the catering cart, and pull the tablecloth closed around you.

6 Ride out with the leftovers.

Ride out with the leftovers.

How to Entertain Yourself During a Meeting

Open a binder in front of you on the table. Behind this barricade, do puzzles, or draw pictures of your officemates as though wearing clown makeup.

HOW TO
DISCREETLY PASS
GAS MID-MEETING

★ Cough loudly.
Cough again and get a drink of water.

★ Yawn and stretch vigorously.

★ Crinkle or tear up a piece of paper.
Show a sign of disgust as you reject the proposal written
on the paper.

★ Applaud vigorously.
Time it correctly so that the moment is appropriate.

★ Laugh loudly.
Pound the table. Snort with laughter.

★ Move your chair to produce loud squeaking noise.

★ Drop a thick report or file on the floor.

★ Call the conference room.
Holding your cell phone under the table, dial the
conference room number and the extension. Wait for
the phone to ring.

Applaud vigorously.

 Deflect the blame.

Glance at a colleague to your right and wrinkle your nose with distaste. Make eye contact with a colleague across the table; slightly incline your head to the right and mouth the word "whoa."

Be Aware

- The techniques outlined can also be used to mask the sounds of burping, stomach growling, or coughing up phlegm.

- Avoid eating these high-risk items before an important meeting to reduce the chance of an "incident": beans, broccoli, cauliflower, carbonated beverages, fatty foods, fresh fruit, onions, and salads.

How to Stifle Uncontrollable Laughter

★ Cough as you are laughing.

★ Stab yourself in the thigh with a pen or pencil.

★ Snap a binder clip closed on your finger.

★ Pull on your necktie.

★ Exit the room.
Excuse yourself and rapidly walk to the bathroom.

How to Take the Last Doughnut

Hold the doughnut aloft and announce "This is the last one. Does anyone want to split this with me?" Touch as much of the doughnut's surface area as possible.

HOW TO MAKE AN IMPROMPTU TOAST

1 Keep it simple.
A toast made in front of colleagues should be brief and safe.

2 Follow the "Past, Present, Future" (PPF) rule.
Acknowledge past successes, present situations, and future objectives. For example: "We've been through a difficult year together, but in the end, we made it a successful one. I can think of no better team to be moving forward with—I love working with all of you. Here's to a bright and successful future together."

3 Avoid problems.
Stay away from losses, morale problems, indictments, former employees, or other natural or human-made disasters. If the last year has been truly horrible, refer to it in a neutral, ambiguous way: "It's been quite a year . . ." or, "As this extraordinary year comes to an end . . ." If the problems are continuing and you don't want to lie, say something emphatic but meaningless: "What a group of people to work with!" or, "I've never worked with a group like this!" or, "The talents and abilities of all of you continue to amaze me!" The future is the easiest portion of the toast, since you can hope and wish without regard to reality. Nonetheless, moderation is best: "The coming year promises to be astonishing!" or, "The sky's the limit in the year ahead."

how to make an impromptu toast

Be brief. No one is really listening.

4 Focus on the people.

Your toast should be about people in general—about spirit, creativity, and bonding—rather than about specific financial results, projects undertaken, or company goals. All of the partygoers are hoping you don't mention them by name, and they really want to get back to eating and drinking.

5 Use humor judiciously.

A little levity may be appreciated, but jokes can slow down your toast and breed restlessness. Depending upon your condition, you may be in no position to gauge what is funny. Attempts at humor could backfire and insult people, open wounds, or just be incomprehensible. If a remark or a joke bombs, keep going. Pausing will only call attention to it and add to the audience's discomfort.

6 **Smile, nod, and look proud as you are speaking.**
Keep your glass raised and lift it even higher as you conclude the toast. Remember, no one is really listening, anyway.

HOW TO REMOVE A TIE CAUGHT IN THE DOCUMENT FEEDER

1 Determine how quickly you will need to act.

If your breathing is constricted, do not hesitate—cut the tie off quickly (see step 5). You may be able to reduce some of the constriction by getting as close to the feeder as possible.

2 If your breathing is not restricted, try pulling the tie.

Use firm but steady pressure. Do not yank: If the document feeder uses gear-driven rollers, you may strip the gears or tear the tie. If the feeder is particularly powerful, you may be unable to pull the tie out.

3 Turn off the copier.

If you can reach the power switch, turn it off. Alternatively, yank or kick out the power cord.

4 Search the area for a cutting implement.

Copier areas often house scissors, utility knives, paper cutters, and other devices you might use to cut the tie free. Open the copier supply door and look in there. Feel around on nearby tables and inside nearby cabinets for useful items.

Turn off machine; cut the tie or call for help.

5 Make a single fast cut across the tie at its shortest visible point.
Pull the tie taut with your neck or free hand, and slice through it quickly.

6 Call for help if you cannot fix the situation yourself.
Cry out for help. If a phone is within reach, call the receptionist or a coworker.

7 If help does not arrive and no cutting implement is available, try to detach the feeder unit.
Often, the feeder unit simply snaps onto the top of the copier. You may be able to lift it off its hinges.

HOW TO RESTORE
A SHREDDED
DOCUMENT

1 Determine the identifying characteristics of the document.
Use paper color and weight, distinctive type fonts, illustrations, and logos to establish which is the document you are trying to restore. Find an unshredded document or letter from the same sender as a model.

2 Sort the shreds.
Using the identifying characteristics of the stationery, and comparing the angle of the edges of each shred, begin to organize the shred strips. Separate and discard shreds from other documents until all remaining shreds are from the target document.

3 Begin paste-up.
Place the first shred vertically on your paste-up board (a whiteboard works well) using clear, removable tape. Using the same orientation, place a second shred alongside the first. Compare it against one side, then the other. If it is a match, tape it down next to the original shred. If it is not, lightly tape it down an inch away, parallel to the first strip.

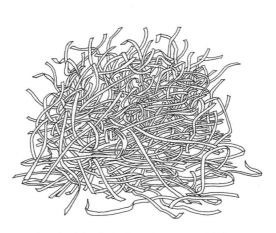

Sort shreds by distinctive color, type, and design.
Discard shreds not from target document.

Tape each shred in place to reassemble document.

4 | Repeat.

Continue comparing strips. Keep the "raw" (uncompared) strips separate from the "rejected" (compared but nonmatching) strips. If you run out of room, use a second paste-up board. Join matching strips as soon as the match is discovered.

5 | Copy the reconstituted document.

When the document is reassembled, sandwich taped strips between two sheets of clear overhead projector film or clear contact paper and photocopy.

Be Aware

• A three-page document will have 100 to 200 shred strips, and reassembly will take 1 to 2 hours, depending on skill level.

• Cross shredders, which shred documents in both directions, make salvage virtually impossible.

SALVAGE A COFFEE-STAINED DOCUMENT

If you are working with a signed contract or a document you cannot replace, you will have to restore the existing pages.

1 | Blot the stain immediately.

Use a clean rag or paper towel to remove as much of the coffee as possible before it dries. Blot, do not wipe. The longer the stain sets, the more difficult the removal.

2 | Examine the stain.
If the stain caused the ink to run, you are probably dealing with an unsalvageable document. Follow the directions in step 3 to be sure.

3 | Determine the printing method.
Wet the end of an ear swab and quickly run it across a nonstained word. If the ink transfers to the cotton, the document was printed on an ink-jet printer and salvage is not possible. Use as is.

4 | Make a vinegar solution.
For a small stain (one to two inches in diameter), mix one tablespoon white vinegar with one tablespoon cold water. (Double or triple the amounts based on stain size.) Pour the mixture into a plate or shallow dish.

5 | Place the stained document on the edge of the dish.
Using a metal spoon, weight the stained portion so it rests in the solution. It is not necessary to immerse the entire sheet.

6 | Soak for 5 minutes.
If the stain is still present, let the document soak for five additional minutes.

7 | Remove from the solution and blot.
Blot the wet area using a clean, dry paper towel. Do not rub.

how to restore a shredded document

8 Dry.

For best results, clip the paper to a string with a clothespin or paper clip to expose both sides to the air. Drying time is about 30 minutes. If time is of the essence or the document is very wrinkled, use a warm iron to carefully smooth the stained area and to speed the drying process.

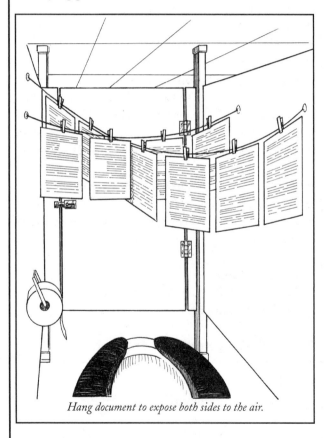

Hang document to expose both sides to the air.

Be Aware

- Do not rub the stained area when the stain is fresh or damp from the vinegar, as you may rip the document.

- Depending on the severity and freshness of the stain, blotting repeatedly with a vinegar-soaked paper towel instead of soaking may be effective for removal. When the stain has faded, blot with a clean, dry paper towel and dry as above.

- If the signature page at the end of a contract is the stained page, do not try to remove the stain. Blot dry and leave alone. The signatories may have used a fountain pen or a type of ink that is water soluble.

HOW TO UNCLOG
THE OFFICE TOILET
WITHOUT A PLUNGER

1 Wait several minutes.
Often clogs will resolve themselves with time.

2 Prepare more water.
Hold a full pitcher of water three feet above the rim of the bowl.

3 Pour and flush.
Pour the water into the bowl as you flush the toilet. The added water and pressure increases the force of the flush.

4 Check the bowl.
If it is still clogged, continue.

5 Get a wire coat hanger.
Untwist the hanger until it is relatively straight.

6 Tie a small hand towel to the hanger.
Create a loop at one end of the hanger to give you a better grip. Tie the hand towel in a knot at the other end. The knot should be approximately the same size as the opening at the bottom of the bowl. Make another small loop in the hanger just below the towel to prevent it from sliding off.

7 Push the hanger through the clog.
Continue pushing as far as you can.

8 Plunge.
Move the hanger up and down and in small circles to clear the clog.

9 Withdraw the hanger.

10 Flush.
If the clog does not clear, wait 10 minutes, then repeat steps 7 through 10. If the water level in the bowl remains high and close to the rim, do not try to flush the toilet.

IF PUSHING THE HANDLE DOES NOT FLUSH THE TOILET

1 Remove the toilet tank lid.
If the toilet does not have a tank—often the case with high-pressure toilets in office buildings—do not try to fix a nonflushing toilet. Just leave and call maintenance.

Check the back of the handle.

2 The handle should be connected inside the tank to one end of the "lift chain," or to a thin rod (float arm) connected to the chain. At its other end, the lift chain should be connected to the toilet flapper. One of the connections is most likely broken.

how to unclog the office toilet without a plunger

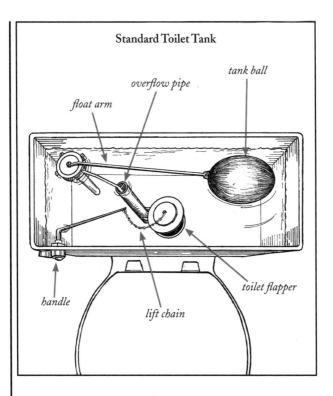

Standard Toilet Tank

tank ball

overflow pipe

float arm

handle

lift chain

toilet flapper

3 Turn off the water.

Turn the water off at the valve just below the tank. Put on a pair of thick rubber gloves.

4 Pull up the lift chain.

Tank water may be contaminated with waste if the trap seal is broken. Using your gloved hand or a hanger, pull up the chain. The toilet will flush. If the water supply is still on, the tank will begin filling quickly, so you will need to work fast.

5 | Reconnect the flapper and chain.
Attach the chain to the handle using a paperclip, safety pin, or twist tie.

6 | Turn the water back on.

7 | Wash your hands thoroughly.
Use antibacterial soap or hydrogen peroxide.

Be Aware

Occasionally the toilet will not flush because the flapper has become dislodged and is not seating properly, causing the water to keep running into the bowl and the tank to remain empty. Jiggle the handle slightly to reseat the flapper properly.

HOW TO SURVIVE IF YOU ARE CAUGHT SLACKING

SURFING THE WEB

⭐ Blame your search engine.
Explain that your search engine mistakenly has provided you with an address to an inappropriate site. Alternatively, claim you made a typing error in the Web address.

⭐ Blame your browser.
Say that someone has set a new "home page" on your Internet browser. Sounding annoyed, loudly ask, "Who keeps setting my browser to open on this sports page? I'm trying to get those new numbers for my report!" You can also claim that you're having trouble loading certain work-related Web sites and so you are visiting more popular sites to see if the computer is working properly.

⭐ Blame the Web site.
Claim that the window with inappropriate material opened unexpectedly while you were viewing something else. Lament that such "pop-ups" are very common and should be regulated.

✪ **Blame an e-mail correspondent.**
Claim that someone sent you the hyperlink, and you clicked it without knowing what it was.

Be Aware
• When surfing the Web, always keep the corporate intranet site up in a separate browser window. Be ready to click over quickly.
• Position your monitor at an angle that prevents anyone standing at the entrance to your office or cube from viewing the screen.

Asleep at Your Desk

✪ **Blame work.**
Say, "I'm so exhausted; I was here until midnight last night!" Do not attempt this if your boss works late and you do not.

✪ **Blame medication.**
Claim that your new allergy medicine has been making you drowsy. Say, "Those antihistamines just knock me out!"

✪ **Blame lunch.**
Say, "Wow, I guess I should not have eaten that turkey sandwich. Triptophan really makes me sleepy!"

how to survive if you are caught slacking

The Proper Napping Position

forehead on fingertips

thumb supporting jaw

arm perpendicular to desk

Be Aware

When taking a nap, always rest your elbow on your desk and keep your arm perpendicular to the desktop. Your forehead should rest on your four fingers—your thumb, spread apart from the fingers, should support your jaw. This position will keep your head up and aimed at your desk. Face in a direction so that it is not immediately visible to someone approaching your desk that your eyes are closed. Keep an important group of documents in your perceived line of sight so as to appear to be reading intently.

HOW TO ENHANCE YOUR STATURE

Pretend You Have an Assistant

⭐ Alter your outgoing voicemail message.
Ask a spouse or friend, preferably with an intriguing foreign accent, to record your outgoing message. It should be a version of the following: "You have reached the office of [your name here]. He is not available to take your call. Please leave a message and he will return your call as soon as possible."

⭐ Receive calls on your mobile phone.
While you are with someone you want to impress, either in an office conference room or at a restaurant, have a friend call you at a prearranged time. Answer the phone and say to the person with whom you are meeting, "Sorry, but I have to take this call. No one but my assistant has this number and I told him to call me only in emergencies."

⭐ Use a pager.
Subscribe to a paging service that alerts you with a beep for headlines or sports scores. Pretend the pages are from your assistant. In an exasperated voice, say, "It's my new assistant. He can't seem to do anything without my approval!"

★ Tip the host at a restaurant.
Tell the host to come to your table during the meal and say that you have an urgent phone call from your assistant.

ATTEND MEETINGS TO WHICH YOU ARE NOT INVITED

★ Ask the receptionist for a conference room reservation schedule.
Determine which meetings are worth crashing.

★ Choose meetings carefully.
Do not attend any meeting at which your direct supervisor is present. If your supervisor is out of the office, definitely attend the meeting and people will think you have been designated as a replacement. If your supervisor is in town, go to other departments' meetings.

★ Invent a reason for attending.
Approach the person running the meeting in advance and explain that you are attending for "professional development." The chairperson will most likely assume that there is some new Human Resources department program. Others attending the meeting will assume you are supposed to be there.

★ Bring snacks.
People will never question your attendance if you bring food.

MOVE INTO AN UNOCCUPIED OFFICE

1 Take note of offices that have been vacant for a significant length of time.

2 Slowly take possession of an office.
Begin by working on a project in the office. If questioned, explain that you "needed a little peace and quiet in order to get [project name] done."

3 Occupy the office regularly.
For two weeks, spend at least an hour a day in the space, working on your project.

4 Expand your hours of occupancy.
After two weeks, begin leaving personal items and other files in the office.

5 Log onto the computer in the new office with your password.

6 Forward your phone calls.
Program your phone to send your calls to the extension in the new office.

7 Complain to the IT department.
Tell the Information Technologies department that your old extension still hasn't been transferred to your new phone.

8 Move your nameplate.
Place your nameplate on the new desk or in the slot outside the door, depending on company practice.

9 Close the door when working.
Look annoyed when anyone knocks or tries to come in. After approximately eight weeks of squatting, the office will be perceived as yours.

ALTER YOUR BUSINESS CARDS

⭐ Count the number of characters in your title.
The new title you select needs to occupy roughly the same space on the card so that it doesn't float or appear obviously doctored. For example, "Editorial Assistant" can become "Editorial Director," but not simply "Editor" or "Senior Editor." Suggested replacements:
- "Marketing Manager" with "Marketing Director"
- "Assistant to the President" with "Assistant Vice-President"
- "Executive Secretary" with "Chief Exec. Officer"
- "Customer Service Rep." with "Customer Service Mgr."

⭐ Use correction fluid, tape, a razor blade, and modified printer labels to add or subtract words and letters from your business card.

Use Props

⭐ Carry a briefcase.

Invest in a good-quality leather briefcase or attaché case and carry it at all times. When someone asks you for something, say, "Oh, I have it here in my briefcase." Consider a locking model for added stature.

⭐ Carry a fountain pen.

Fountain pens denote wealth and good breeding. Do not carry the pen in a pocket protector.

Look Busier than You Are

⭐ Purchase a headset and attach it to your phone.

It doesn't matter whether it's actually connected or not—tape it to the bottom of the phone if it won't hook in. Wear it constantly, and talk loudly whenever someone passes by.

⭐ Keep large piles of paper on your desk at all times. Rearrange the stacks occasionally.

⭐ Type furiously from time to time.

Position your monitor so the screen is not visible to anyone passing by or entering your space. Periodically, look intently at the monitor and type as fast as you can. Type nonsense, if you must—but do it at a speed of at least 70 words per minute.

★ Show up early and stay late.

You can maintain the same eight-hour day—just run your errands in the middle of the day. Few people will think twice about your absence from your desk in the middle of the day, but everyone will notice how early you get there and how late you leave. Long midday absences, if noticed, will be interpreted as business lunches, a sign of importance.

★ Muss your hair and look stressed whenever you pass your supervisor's office.

START A HELPFUL RUMOR

★ Receive messages from headhunters.

Have a friend, posing as a headhunter, make repeated calls to the receptionist. The friend should say, "I'm with [official sounding name] Headhunting Agency— may I speak with [your name]?" Word will likely get back to your supervisor.

★ Plant a reference check with the Human Resources department.

When the office is sure to be closed—late at night, on a weekend, or when you are certain everyone in the Human Resources department has left for the day— have a friend leave a voice-mail message saying he or she is checking references on [your name] and will call back later. The caller should not leave a return phone number nor a company name, but can leave their own name. The caller should sound casual but busy, as if he or she is checking a list of names with a variety of employers.

★ **Take the receptionist or your direct supervisor's assistant into your "confidence."**
Explain that you are "entertaining" a position at another company, but that you "really want to stay." Ask for advice, knowing that word will get back to the boss.

★ **Talk with people in other departments about forthcoming changes in your department.**
Say you are not at liberty to reveal the whole story, but major changes will be coming. Ask if they know anything about future plans for your supervisor's parking place/office.

★ **Conduct rumor-inducing conversations in public areas.**
Spend time conversing at the water cooler, the lunchroom, bathroom, lobby, stairwells, elevators, and hallways. A loud whisper is most effective in getting people's attention. What you are talking about is not important: The fact that you are engaging in so many hushed conversations is the important factor.

HOW TO AVOID DOWNSIZING

MAKE YOURSELF SEEM INDISPENSABLE

⭐ **Perform thankless tasks.**
Offer to do the billing, track vacation or comp time, sort the mail, answer the phones at lunchtime, replace the toner, or clean out the refrigerator. Master the jobs no one else wants.

⭐ **Offer to organize office social events.**
Do more than your share of planning office birthday parties and making sure everyone signs the card. Organize office parties, picnics, and holiday gatherings. Maintain a password-protected database of contacts and suppliers.

⭐ **Get your name out.**
Write an occasional article for the company newsletter or speak at a company event.

⭐ **Become the key master.**
Cultivate a collection of keys and codes for as many doors and drawers as possible. Store them in a locked place.

⭐ **Be the one at meetings who says, "OK, let's get started."**

★ Be the office handyperson.
Bring your tool kit to work and fix little problems around the office.

★ Propose ways to save the company money.
Suggest that employees use second-day postage rather than express; turn off lights in unused offices; reuse sticky notes; recycle memos, reports, and other documents internally by using the back side for scrap paper and drafts; insert "saving the resources of our company and our country" into every conversation; and remind your boss that "a dollar not spent goes right to the bottom line."

★ Start wearing glasses.
You will look more intelligent.

HOW TO SURVIVE A NIGHTMARE BUSINESS TRIP

FLYING IN COACH

1 Be prepared.
Take supplies with you to make the flight more pleasant:
- Good food. Coach-class meals have never been stellar, and you're guaranteed a good meal if you bring something good onboard. Plus, you can eat whenever you wish.
- Neck pillow. The inflatable pillow makes sleeping and even sitting much more comfortable.
- Water. Avoid becoming dehydrated by the plane's air conditioning system.
- Lip balm. Avoid uncomfortable and unsightly chapped lips.

2 Get a seat with extra legroom.
The bulkheads and exit rows usually offer the most room to stretch out. A middle seat in an exit row may be more comfortable than an aisle seat in a nonexit row. Make sure, however, that the seatbacks recline—certain exit rows have nonreclining chairs.

3 Request a seat at the rear of the plane, in a row with open seats.

The rear is not only the safest area in the event of a crash, but it will allow you to board immediately after the first-class passengers, giving you the first available access to the overhead storage bins as well as pillows and blankets. Open seats will allow you to stretch out. Choose a window seat. If you sit on the aisle, you risk being disturbed every time someone in your row wants to get up or every time a person passes on the way to the lavatory. With a window seat, you'll be in control of the shade and have a wall to lean against.

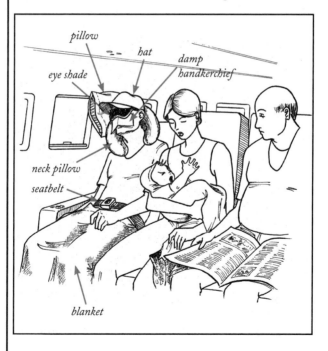

4 Place your carry-on bag in the overhead compartment.

Keep the space under the seat in front of you clear, so you can stretch. If there is no room in the overhead compartment for your bag, place it under another open seat on your row. If you must stash it beneath the seat in front of you, plan to use it as a footrest by pulling it out slightly.

5 Make yourself comfortable.

Remove your shoes, as feet tend to expand slightly during flight. Recline your seat to a comfortable position. Lift the between-seat armrest to give yourself a little extra room if you have an empty seat next to you. Place an inflatable neck pillow around your neck, or use an airline pillow. Lean against the wall of the plane.

6 When the seatbelt sign is turned off, move about the cabin.

Walk and stretch in the galley area to keep your legs from stiffening and to prevent blood clots from forming.

7 When sleeping, insert cotton in your ears and place a moist handkerchief over your nose.

Low-level engine noise can disrupt sleep patterns. For better rest, filter out noise using sterile cotton instead of ear plugs, so the inner ear can adjust to cabin pressure changes. If sterile cotton is not available, use noise-canceling headphones connected to a CD or MP3 player. A damp handkerchief over your nose will prevent your nasal passages from drying out. Block out as much of the light as possible. Close the window shade. Don an eye mask, or use an article of clothing (sweater, jacket, hat) as a blindfold.

8 | Use deep-breathing techniques to relax.
Breathe in deeply through your nose, then out through your mouth. Focus only on the breaths you are taking—say to yourself, "Sleeeeeeeep. Sleeeeeeep. Sleeeeeep," as you inhale and exhale. Do not think about work, about your big meeting tomorrow, about how much you would rather be at home—think only about sleep.

Be Aware
Keep your seatbelt visible at all times. If your seatbelt is not in plain sight, you risk being awakened by the flight crew for a belt check.

LOST LUGGAGE

1 | File a report at the airport.
As soon as you realize your bags are missing, go immediately to the lost-luggage counter and file a report. Get a copy of the report, and write down the name of the person who helps you and the report number.

2 | Obtain the direct phone number for the baggage counter.
Airport personnel may give you a toll-free number to call to check on the status of your bags. Take the

number, but ask for the number of the lost-baggage counter at the airport itself.

3 | Request compensation.
Some airlines will issue a check on the spot to cover the immediate cost of your buying clothing or essentials. Or the airline may give you a toiletries bag to cover your grooming needs until your bag is retained.

4 | Call the airport baggage counter regularly.
Do not assume the airline will call you.

5 | Be prepared for a two-day delay.
Do not assume that your bag will be put on the next departing flight to your destination: Airlines place recovered luggage only on their own planes, not on those of other carriers. If the next flight is not until late the following evening, you may not see your bag for two days.

6 | Purchase necessary items before you leave the airport.
If you arrive at your destination on a holiday or late at night, you may not be able to shop for essentials in town.

Be Aware

- If luggage is lost rather than just delayed, an airline's liability in the United States is limited to $1,250 per passenger, no matter how many bags have been lost. On international flights, the liability limit is about $9 per pound of checked baggage. Reimbursement may take months.

- To make your bag easier to spot, place a colored ribbon on the handle or a distinctive strap around the bag before checking it.

- Watch the bags as they come down the conveyer belt to the carousel, even if you do not have immediate access to it. You will be able to see if anyone else takes your bag.

- Write your name and the phone number of the place you will be staying for the first two days of your trip on two business cards. Place one inside your luggage and one in a card holder on the outside of your bag. (Never place your home address and phone in a visible identification tag. You do not want to advertise that you are away from home.)

- Dress for the worst—wear clothing on the plane that you can live in (and with) for two days. Anticipate that you might be giving your presentation or attending the meeting in what you are wearing on the plane.

- Carry essential medical and hygiene items, as well as any irreplaceable presentation materials, in your carry-on luggage.

CHEAP HOTEL

1 Request a room with a quiet location.
Avoid rooms near elevators, vending machines, the ice maker, the parking lot, or a noisy bar. Ask for a room at the end of the hall so there is less foot traffic outside the door.

2 Check the mechanicals and plumbing.
Before unpacking, check air conditioning, heat, television, lights, and water pressure. If any are not working properly or are otherwise unacceptable, request a new room.

3 Remove the bedspread.
Cheap hotels do not regularly clean bedspreads. Use towels for warmth. Call the front desk to request extra towels if there aren't enough in the room.

4 Clip the curtains closed.
If the curtains do not fully close, secure the two sides together using whatever you have on hand—paper or binder clips, tape, or pins and needles from a sewing kit.

5 Check the mattress firmness.
If the bed is too soft, place the mattress on the floor.

6 Check the clock.
Make sure the alarm is not set to go off in the middle of the night. Avoid the wake-up service—it is

notoriously unreliable in cheap hotels. Set the alarm clock, or carry a travel clock with an alarm.

7 | Avoid the morning shower rush.
Cheap hotels may run out of hot water anytime between 7 and 9 A.M. Shower earlier or later.

Be Aware
- Travel with lightbulbs bright enough to use for reading.
- Travel with two small rubber doorstops. For security, wedge one firmly under the door to your room and the other under the door that adjoins the next room.
- Travel with snacks, including protein bars and instant hot cereal. Cheap hotels may have no restaurant, no in-room coffee, and no vending machines. Even if there is a restaurant, the food might be terrible.

DULL TOWN

⭐ | Ask the locals for recommendations.
Ask the hotel clerk (or better yet, a porter) for a restaurant where you can "sample the local flavor." Most towns have at least one dish, restaurant, or tourist attraction that residents consider special.

⭐ | Adopt an alias.
Pretend to be someone else when you go out. Be a secret service agent, an astronaut, a mime—whatever

your fantasy is. Pretend you have an accent. Cross-dressing is not recommended for all towns, however.

★ **Do the opposite of everything you normally do.**
If you usually go to bed early, stay out late. If you usually drink beer, drink coffee. Talk to the people you would normally ignore or avoid.

★ **Play cards.**
If none of the above works, obtain a deck of cards. Solitaire is a great time killer. Build a house of cards, or try to toss as many as you can across the room and into the wastebasket.

HOW TO VIDEO-CONFERENCE FROM THE BEACH

1 Dress your upper body appropriately.
Wear a shirt, buttoned all the way up. Add a necktie, sweater, or blazer over the shirt. Shave and/or put on makeup. Brush and comb your hair. Remove sunglasses or goggles. Remove zinc oxide and suntan lotion from the bridge of your nose.

2 Keep your lower body out of the frame.
Before linking to the meeting, zoom the digital video camera in tightly, so that you can only be seen from your ribcage up.

3 Employ props.
Hold a pen. Once every five or ten minutes, tap it thoughtfully against your chin. Clutch papers in your hand and occasionally bring them up into the frame; when they are not in the frame, occasionally rustle them. Pour your piña colada into a coffee cup and periodically sip it (remove the straw).

4 Create a background.
Take cushions from lounge chairs and prop them up behind you, creating the impression that you are sitting on a sofa. If you have called in sick, scatter a

Keep your lower body out of the frame. Employ props.

thermometer, hot water bottle, a tissue box, and aspirin containers around the cushions.

5 **Wear a microphone.**
Clip a cheap microphone to your collar, as close as possible to your mouth to drown out any stray background noise, such as waves crashing on the beach, or children laughing.

6 | Participate in the meeting.

7 | Sit up straight.
Leaning to one side will reveal the panoramic ocean vista.

8 | Do not fall asleep.
If you drift off, you may slump out of frame and reveal your tropical surroundings.

9 | Experience technical problems.
With your big toe, reach forward and shut off your laptop.

10 | Go for a swim.

11 | Send an e-mail to your boss.
Explain that your connection must have been lost. Apologize. Ask that someone send you information on what you missed from the rest of the meeting.

12 | Go for another swim.

CHAPTER 6

OUT AND ABOUT

HOW TO
DRIVE A TANK

1 Survey the area.

Evaluate the immediate surrounding area before enter-ing the tank, since the field of vision is limited once inside. Note obstacles or unstable ground and steep slopes or banks, which can cause the vehicle to roll.

2 Board the tank.

Use the skirt step on the left front of most tanks to climb onto the front of the tank. Locate the driver's hatch, below the turret. Lift and swing the hatch to the side, locking it in the open position. Climb inside. Close and lock the hatch behind you.

3 Sit down.

The driver's seat, located in the center of the space, is tilted back like a dentist's chair to accommodate the driving area's low ceiling. Adjust the angle and height of the seat until you are comfortable and can see through the periscopes directly in front of your seat and can reach the controls.

4 Identify the gauges and instruments.

Your driver's master control panel sits to your right and instrument panel to your left. The instrument panel features your fuel level indicator and other gauges while the control panel holds the switches and knobs necessary to turn on the tank's engines, fans, and other

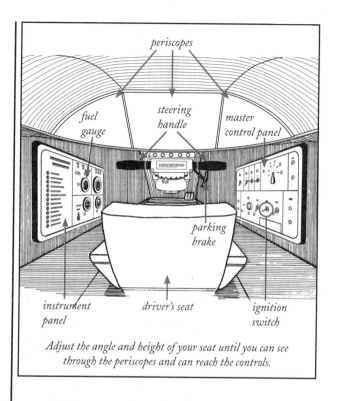

periscopes

steering
handle

fuel
gauge

master
control panel

parking
brake

instrument
panel

driver's seat

ignition
switch

*Adjust the angle and height of your seat until you can see
through the periscopes and can reach the controls.*

systems. The controls and gauges are clearly marked.
The gearshift is located atop the steering handle in
front of you.

5 Check the fuel gauge.

Examine the fuel gauge on the instrument panel to
your left to determine whether you have enough fuel
to start the tank and reach your destination. Tank
fuel consumption is measured in gallons per mile. You
will need 10 gallons just to start the engine and about

2 gallons per mile once you get going. You can travel about 300 miles on a full tank of fuel.

6 Start the tank.
Flip the silver ignition switch at the bottom left-center of your control panel up to the "On" position. The engine will need about three to five minutes to warm up. You can help speed the process by revving the engine, twisting back the throttle on the right steering grip as you would on a motorcycle grip.

7 Test the periscopes.
The driver's visual system consists of three periscopes that look like windshields. The two on either side of you allow you to view in front of the tank and to its left and right for about a 120-degree visual field. In between those two periscopes, you will find a central image-intensifying periscope, which looks straight ahead, for use in driving at night or in smoky or dusty situations.

8 Release the parking brake.
The parking brake control is to the right of your steering handle. Pull on its black, T-shaped handle, twist and ease it downward to release it.

9 Put the tank into gear.
Pull the silver transmission selector knob above the steering handle and ease it into the D (Drive) slot, second from the right.

10 Start slowly.

Some tanks can accelerate from 0 to 45 mph in under 10 seconds. Ease the throttle back to move ahead, slowly at first, twisting back further as you feel more comfortable with handling the tank at higher speeds.

11 Steer.

Guide the tank as you would a bicycle, snowmobile, or motorcycle by rotating the steering handlebar to the left and right.

12 Listen for tread buildup.

The tank's treads can become disabled with debris. If the tank is not responding quickly to your steering, you may have mud, sand, or some other substance built up on your tracks, which can cause the treads to come off the wheels, leaving the tank essentially immobilized. This buildup is usually accompanied by a popping sound. Drive the tank forward in a straight line over level ground until the popping stops, indicating that the tracks have cleared themselves.

13 Brake.

Once you have arrived at your destination, come to a stop by easing your foot all the way down on the service brake located on the floor beneath your steering handle. Before exiting the tank, reapply the parking brake by pulling the black T-shaped handle to your right.

Be Aware

- Put on protective headgear before entering the tank. Tank interiors are full of levers, knobs, and other protruding objects that can cut, burn, or daze.
- Never try to get onto and into a tank while it is in motion, no matter how slowly it is moving.
- Wear earplugs or noise-canceling headphones. Tank engines are loud.
- Run the exhaust fan for at least five minutes for every hour on board to replenish the tank's limited oxygen supply.
- Tank interiors can be claustrophobic and nauseating, as they tend to fill with overpowering odors from their huge engines. Skip your previous meal before your tank ride.

HOW TO PARALLEL PARK A TRACTOR TRAILER

1 Pull ahead of the space you want.

Find a parking space that is one and a half times the length of your truck. (If your truck is 20 feet long, your space should be 30 feet long). Pull up ahead of the space, leaving at least two arm lengths of space between you and the car or truck next to you.

2 Turn on your emergency lights.

3 Back up.

As you put the truck in reverse, give three short horn blasts to alert anyone on the street behind you.

4 Stop.

When, in your curb-side mirror, you see the front end of your truck's trailer even with the rear bumper of the car or truck in front of your chosen space, brake and put the truck back in drive.

5 Turn the wheel.

Turn the wheel of the tractor away from the curb as far as possible.

how to parallel park a tractor trailer

*Swing the tractor out into the roadway as you back
the trailer into the spot.*

6 | Swing out.
Check for oncoming traffic, and then apply gas, swinging the tractor out into the roadway as you back the trailer into the spot. (The trailer will move in the opposite direction that you are turning the wheel).

7 | Cut back.
When the back curbside wheel of the trailer hits the curb, stop, turn the wheel all the way in the other direction, and pull forward.

8 | Repeat steps 6 and 7.
Check both side-mirrors to gauge the position of the trailer. If the mirror's blind spot keeps you from seeing the exact position of the trailer, get out of the truck, walk around, and look. Repeat steps 6 and 7 until the trailer is well into the spot and the tractor is not jutting out into the road. Trailers are not designed to go efficiently in reverse and may need dozens of small adjustments to be navigated properly into the space.

9 | Double check your curb distance and ramp room.
Maneuver the tractor until it is no further than 18 inches from the curb, and the back end is at least 18 feet from the car or truck behind it, so the ramp can come down and moving trolleys can get in and out. If your distances are insufficient, pull out from the space and start again.

Be Aware

- The narrower the street, the less room you will have to swing out your tractor in step 6. If you are parking on a two- or three-lane street, without minimal oncoming traffic, leave more space between your truck and the car next to you, and swing out further.

- Before attempting to navigate city streets in a moving truck, know the height of your vehicle. When approaching overhanging tree branches, ease forward very slowly to avoid damage to the truck or tree. Do not drive under low-hanging power lines.

- Many municipalities require you to give advance notice to the police department to park a moving truck or other tractor trailer for even a short period of time.

HOW TO TELL IF YOUR CAR HAS BEEN TAMPERED WITH

1 | Examine the ground around your car.
Get down on all fours and crawl along the ground around your car up to a distance of 25 feet away, looking for small bits of wire or wire insulation, discarded scraps of tape, or puttylike lumps.

2 | Examine the locks and windows.
Run a flashlight along the cracks between the doors and the doorframes, looking for small wires. Using a magnifying glass, examine the door locks and windows, and the area directly surrounding them, for scrapes or scratches indicating forced entry. Check the seam around the trunk; open the trunk and make sure the mats have not been moved, and there are no unfamiliar objects or bits of wire or wire insulation.

3 | Examine the gas tank.
Run your hands over the crack between the gas tank cover to make sure it's flush and shows no signs of prying. Use a magnifying glass to look for scuff marks or scratches. Open the gas tank cover and sniff the tank for strong, nongas odors.

4 | Open the hood.
Shine your flashlight around the engine block, particularly the wiring, to see if anything is disconnected or if there are any new wires present. Run the light along the firewall (the back wall of the engine, separating the fuel tank from the passenger compartment) to make sure it has not been sabotaged.

5 | Use a mirror to examine the underside of the car.
Slide a small handheld mirror under the chassis and slowly move it clockwise around the underside of the car, examining the reflected image for foreign objects attached to the vehicle.

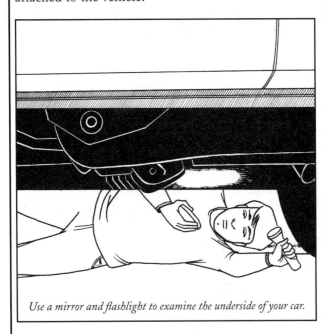

Use a mirror and flashlight to examine the underside of your car.

6 Check your brakes.
Lie down a foot away from the front of the car and sweep your flashlight underneath it, looking for a puddle of greasy liquid, which may be brake fluid that has been drained from your vehicle. Run one finger slowly along the brake lines, from each brake pad back to the master cylinder, feeling for pinholes or cuts.

7 Look into the exhaust pipe.
Shine a flashlight into the pipe to look for foreign objects.

8 Inspect your wheels and tires.
Run your hands all the way around each tire to feel for minor punctures or small slashes. Feel each lug nut to make sure it is still properly tightened. Check the air pressure of each tire with a tire pressure gauge to make sure no one has let the air out of your tires.

9 Examine the front seats for signs of intrusion.
Before opening the car door, look through the window for signs that someone has been in the car. Note whether the angle of the seats has been altered, if the rearview mirror has been redirected, or if the floor mats have been moved or disturbed.

10 Take a deep breath.
Once settled in the driver's seat, sniff the air. The odor of gasoline within the vehicle can indicate that the gas tank has been tampered with or punctured.

11 Look for a planted device.

Run your fingers along the underside of the passenger and driver's seats in search of foreign objects. Check under the brake and acceleration pedals. Do not apply pressure to the seats until you are satisfied there is nothing beneath them that may be pressure-triggered.

Be Aware

- The best way to notice any tampering is to know your vehicle well under normal circumstances. Carry a photograph of the inside of your engine so you can check the arrangement of wires against the picture before starting your car each time.
- Always leave objects on your front seat, such as newspapers or tissue boxes, so you can gauge whether someone has moved them when you return to the car.

HOW TO DEAL WITH A QUADRUPLE BLOWOUT

1 Hold steering wheel firmly.

Though the car will become increasingly difficult to control, concentrate on keeping the car moving in a straight line. Grasp the steering wheel tightly—it will be shaking violently.

2 Put your hazard lights on.

Your hazards will signal drivers behind you that you are in distress.

3 Apply the brakes.

Put light but steady pressure on the brake pedal to reduce speed. Though the tires are blown, you should still have some tread remaining on each wheel for a few minutes. The "contact patches" (the section of each tire in contact with the road surface) will be greatly reduced, however, and will continue to shrink as pieces of the tire spin off the wheel. The smaller the contact patch, the less friction available to the brakes, less stopping power, and more possibility of spinning out of control. The car will be shaking, along with the steering wheel, and the vehicle will become progressively harder to control.

4 Steer toward a safe stopping point.

Scan the road ahead. Look for a relatively open, flat area on the shoulder. If you are in the center or inside lane, signal and move to the outer lane, but make a gradual lane change with no sudden inputs to the steering wheel. If you cannot see or cannot immediately reach a stopping point, see "How to Continue Driving on Four Blown Tires," below.

5 Let the car roll to a stop.

Once you reach a safe area out of the flow of traffic, take your foot off the brake and allow the car to coast to a stop.

How to Continue Driving on Four Blown Tires

1 Go straight.

If you are on a bridge or stretch of road where you cannot stop safely, keep the car moving in a straight line for as long as possible. Driving on four blown tires, and, eventually, four rims, will be similar to driving on ice: You will have very little stopping power, and the car will tend to spin as you enter turns.

2 Accelerate smoothly.

Less friction with the road surface increases the likelihood of spinning wheels, which will make fast acceleration impossible. Apply the throttle (gas pedal) smoothly and sparingly and only to maintain control while moving in a straight line or through a very gradual turn. Most

Stay on the roadway at all costs.

front-wheel-drive cars have an open differential, where the wheel with the least resistance gets the power. As the tires disintegrate, the wheel with less friction will spin, and the car will swerve from side to side.

Stay on a paved surface.

3 Avoid driving the car off the roadway at all costs. With no rubber remaining, the metal wheels will readily bite into soft ground and cause the car to flip.

4 | Listen for the last pieces of rubber to fly off the wheels.

The car will shake increasingly violently as the tires disintegrate, and you will hear very loud flapping sounds from the corners. The tread will not stay centered on the wheel, and the contact patch will shift wildly, making the car difficult to control. After a mile or two, the last pieces of rubber will come off, and the flapping sound will disappear. Provided the shredded tires have not gotten caught in the wheel wells, driving on the metal rims should provide less shaking and more control. Your contact area with the road, however, will be extremely small (the width of two pencils for each wheel) and traction will be severely limited. The rims will spark as you drive on them.

5 | Pull over as soon as possible.

Eventually, the rims will flatten or crack and the bottom of the car will begin dragging on the road until the friction stops your progress. Steel wheels will last longer and go further than aluminum or magnesium wheels, which are lighter, more brittle, and have a tendency to bend and break under stress.

Be Aware

Run-flat tires have reinforced sidewalls that will support the weight of the car and allow driving with a puncture. However, tires that are severely punctured by treadles or road spikes will begin to shred, and the sidewalls will eventually separate from the tread and come off.

How to Improvise a Driver's Sunshade

Unroll the driver's side window ½ inch. Remove your jacket, shirt, or blouse. Tuck it evenly across the top of the window, then close the window to hold the garment in place to block harsh sunlight. Lift the garment for visibility when changing lanes in that direction.

Junk in the Trunk:
Must-Have Emergency Items

- Local map, atlas, or GPS system
- Crank or battery-powered radio and batteries
- Large flashlight and batteries
- Matches or lighter
- Basic automotive tool kit
- First-aid kit
- Emergency flares
- Spare tire
- Jack
- Jumper cables
- 3 days worth of nonperishable food
- 6 quarts of water per adult passenger
- Duct tape
- Pepper spray, emergency whistle
- Collapsible shovel
- Ice scraper, rock salt (for cold weather)
- Insulated sleeping bag
- 2 two-by-fours
- Rain poncho and boots
- License and registration
- Phone charger
- Emergency roadside assistance phone number
- Bribe money

HOW TO SURVIVE BEING STRANDED IN THE SNOW

1 Get as far off the road as possible.
Drive or push your vehicle fully clear of the roadway, but be sure that your car is still visible to any vehicles that may pass by and be able to offer assistance.

2 Make your car visible to potential rescuers.
Turn on your emergency flashers. When the snow stops falling, raise the car's hood to signal distress; when snow begins to fall again, close the hood. Set up flares along the roadside between your car and the road. Hang a brightly colored cloth such as a red scarf or a torn-off piece of blanket from the antenna.

3 Spell out HELP in the snow.
Use rocks and sticks to spell the word HELP in six-foot-long block letters next to the car so your position is visible from the air.

4 Stay near the car.
Do not leave the vicinity of your vehicle unless help is visible within 100 yards. Blowing and drifting snow can be extremely disorienting, causing you to wander away from your car deeper into the snow and become lost. Shelter is your most important priority in inclement weather.

how to survive being stranded in the snow

Spell out "HELP" in the snow with rocks and sticks.

5 Put on all available clothing.
If traveling with clothes, put them on in layers. Wrap yourself in blankets stored in the trunk. Strip the leather or vinyl from your seats and wrap yourself in them.

6 Run the engine for 10 minutes once an hour.
Clear snow from the exhaust pipe and crack one upwind window to keep carbon monoxide from building up in the car. While the engine is running, turn on the heater to keep body temperature above 90 degrees, warding off hypothermia and frostbite.

7 Remain active.
While sitting in the car, periodically rotate your torso from side to side and move your arms and legs to keep blood flow moving.

8 Huddle for warmth.
If traveling with others, sit in a row in the back seat, wrapping your arms and legs together to stay warm. Take turns sleeping.

9 Forage.
If the snow stops, walk 50 yards along the shoulder in either direction of your car in search of water, cast-off fast food containers, edible plants, or road kill. Never let your vehicle out of sight.

10 Eat snow.
Keep hydrated by eating chunks of the cleanest snow you can find.

11 Build a tire signal fire.

Remove the spare tire from the trunk, or remove one tire from the wheel of the car using a tire jack. Set the tire on the roadway or on the ground near the road cleared of snow. Fill up the center of the tire with dry sticks and paper products from your car and ignite it with the car's cigarette lighter or any other means of ignition. Keep the fire burning with paper products until the fire achieves the 400 degrees necessary to ignite the tire itself. Once lit, a tire will produce a thick black smoke. Do not inhale the smoke, as it contains carbon monoxide, sulfur dioxide, and numerous other toxic chemicals.

Be Aware

- Symptoms of carbon monoxide poisoning include chest tightness, fatigue, dizziness, vomiting, and muscle weakness.

- If afflicted with hypothermia or frostbite, do not drink caffeine or alcohol. Caffeine will amplify the negative effects of cold on the body, while alcohol can slow the heart and restrict blood flow.

- Before setting out in winter conditions, stock your trunk with snow chains, bottled water, food, blankets, and signal flares.

- Only burn your tires if you have exhausted every effort to restart your vehicle, and no vehicles have come by in 48 hours.

HOW TO SURVIVE A LIGHTNING STORM ON A MOUNTAINSIDE

1 Recognize the signs of an approaching storm.
Typical visual cues like cloud cover and light flashes may be obscured by the terrain, tree cover, or your location. Other signs of electrical storms include the smell of ozone, a buzzing sound in the air, or hair that stands up straight. A halo of light known as St. Elmo's fire may be apparent around trees or people.

2 Break away from the group.
If everyone gets struck at once, no one will be able to help the victims.

3 Remove any jewelry or metal on your body.
If your backpack has a metal frame, take off the backpack.

4 Seek a dry, safe shelter.
If you are surrounded by trees, position yourself among the shortest trees in the vicinity. Stay away from trees scarred by previous lightning strikes. If the mountainside is bare, retreat to a lower position if there is time. Avoid overhangs and ridgelines. Try to find a slight bump in the mountainside that will elevate

open mouth

keep hands
off ground

crouch on
balls of feet

insulate feet
from ground

remove
all metal

*Position yourself on a slight bump to interrupt
the path the electricity would travel.*

chapter 6: out and about

you—but only slightly—from the path electricity will likely travel if lightning strikes the ground nearby. A dry cave that is deeper than its mouth is wide is also a good location to wait out the storm.

5 Separate yourself from the ground.
Place insulators like wood, rubber, plastic, or natural (not synthetic) cloth on the ground in your sheltered location.

6 Make yourself as small a target as possible.
Crouch on the balls of your feet on top of the insulation. Put your head down and keep your mouth open to protect your eardrums. Do not put your hands on the ground.

7 After the storm passes, assess whether anyone in your group has been hit.
Common indications that someone has been struck by lightning include temporary hearing loss, dilated pupils, amnesia, paralysis, confusion, weak pulse at the extremities, and irregular heartbeat. If the victim is unconscious, make sure he or she is breathing and perform CPR if necessary. Seek medical attention as soon as possible.

HOW TO SURVIVE WHEN LOST IN THE MOUNTAINS

The number one cause of death when lost in the mountains is hypothermia—humans are basically tropical animals. Staying calm in the face of darkness, loneliness, and the unknown will greatly increase your chances of survival. Eighty percent of mountain survival is your reaction to fear, 10 percent is your survival gear, and the other 10 percent is knowing how to use it. Always tell someone else where you are going and when you will return.

1 Do not panic.
If you told someone where you were going, search and rescue teams will be looking for you. (In general, teams will search only during daylight hours for adults, but will search around the clock for children who are alone.)

2 Find shelter, and stay warm and dry.
Exerting yourself unnecessarily—like dragging heavy logs to build a shelter—will make you sweat and make you cold. Use the shelter around you before trying to construct one. If you are in a snow-covered area, you may be able to dig a cave in deep snow for shelter and protection from the wind. A snow trench may be a better idea—it requires less exertion. Simply use

In snow-covered country, build a snow cave or a snow trench for shelter and warmth. Use dead leaves and branches for insulation.

something to dig a trench, get in it, and cover it with branches or leaves. You should attempt to make your shelter in the middle of the mountain if possible. Stay out of the valleys—cold air falls, and the valley floor can be the coldest spot on the mountain.

3 Signal rescuers for help.

The best time to signal rescuers is during the day, with a signaling device or three fires in a triangle. Signal for help from the highest point possible—it will be easier for rescuers to see you, and any sound you make will travel farther. Build three smoky fires and put your blanket—gold side facing out, if it is a space blanket—on the ground.

4 Do not wander far.

It will make finding you more difficult, as search teams will be trying to retrace your path and may miss you if you have gone off in a different direction. Searchers often wind up finding a vehicle with no one in it because the driver has wandered off.

5 If you get frostbite, do not rewarm the affected area until you're out of danger.

You can walk on frostbitten feet, but once you warm the area and can feel the pain, you will not want to walk anywhere. Try to protect the frostbitten area and keep it dry until you are rescued.

How to Prepare

You must dress properly before entering a wilderness area. Layer your clothing in the following manner:

FIRST (INNER) LAYER: long underwear, preferably polypropylene. This provides only slight insulation—its purpose is to draw moisture off your skin.

SECOND (MIDDLE) LAYER: something to trap and create warm "dead air" space, such as a down parka.

THIRD (OUTER) LAYER: a Gore-Tex or other brand of breathable jacket that allows moisture out but not in. Dry insulation is key to your survival. Once you are wet, it is very difficult to get dry.

Make sure you have the following items in your survival kit, and that you know how to use them (reading the instructions for the first time in the dark wilderness is not recommended):

A HEAT SOURCE. Bring several boxes of waterproof matches, as well as a lighter. Trioxane—a small, light, chemical heat source that the Army uses—is recommended. Trioxane packs can be picked up in outdoor and military surplus stores. Dryer lint is also highly flammable and very lightweight.

SHELTER. Carry a small space blanket, which has a foil-like coating that insulates you. Get one that is silver on one side (for warmth) and orange-gold on the other, which can be used for signaling. The silver side is not a good color to signal with. It can be mistaken for ice or mineral rock. The orange-gold color does not occur in nature and will not be mistaken for anything else.

A SIGNALING DEVICE. A small mirror works well, as do flares or a whistle, which carries much farther than a voice.

FOOD. Pack carbohydrates: bagels, trail mix, granola bars, and so on. Proteins need heat to break down and require more water for digestion.

HOW TO BUILD
A SHELTER IN
THE SNOW

BUILDING A SNOW TRENCH

1 Map out a trench so that the opening is at a right angle to the prevailing wind.

You need to find a space large enough so that the width and length are just a bit longer and taller than your body when lying down. You need only a minimal depth to maintain a cozy space for body heat conservation.

2 Dig the trench with a wider, flatter opening on one end for your head, using whatever tools you have or can create.

A cooking pan or long, flat piece of wood works well as an entrenching tool.

3 Cover the top of the trench with layers of branches, then a tarp, plastic sheeting, or whatever is available, then a thin layer of snow.

A "door" can be made using a backpack, blocks of snow, or whatever materials provide some ventilation and yet block the heat-robbing effects of the wind.

Building a Snow Cave

1 Find a large snowdrift or snowbank on a slope.
Plan your cave with the opening at a right angle to the prevailing wind.

2 Dig a narrow tunnel into the slope (toward the back of the slope) and slightly upward.
Create a cavern big enough to lie in without touching the sides, roof, or ends.

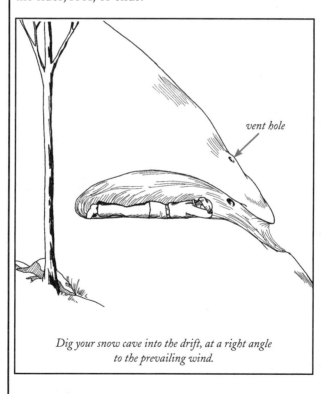

vent hole

Dig your snow cave into the drift, at a right angle to the prevailing wind.

3 Make the ceiling slightly dome-shaped.
A flat ceiling has no strength and will in most cases collapse before you are finished digging. The roof should be at least 12 inches thick. If you can see blue-green light (from filtered sunlight) through the top, the roof is too thin.

4 Put a small vent hole in the roof.
The hole will provide fresh air and a vent for a candle, if you are going to use one. Do not add any heat source larger than a small candle. Excessive heat will cause the ceiling to soften, drip, and weaken.

BUILDING A QUIN-ZHEE

If snow depth is minimal and you have a lot of time and energy, build a Quin-Zhee. A Quin-Zhee is a snow shelter that was developed by the Athabascan Indians, who lived mainly in Canada and Alaska.

1 Pile up a very large mound of packed snow.
The pile needs to be big enough for you to sit or lie down comfortably inside when it is hollowed out.

2 Wait an hour for the snow to consolidate.

3 Dig in and build a snow cave.

Be Aware

- A preferable alternative to building a snow shelter is a man-made structure or vehicle. If none is available, search for anything that will help protect your body from heat loss. Caves, downed timber, or rock outcroppings can help protect you from the elements.
- If you cannot stay dry in the process of building a snow shelter, or you cannot get dry after you have built it, do not build it! Moving enough snow to create a shelter big enough for even just one person is hard work, and any contact of your skin or clothing with snow while digging will amplify your body's heat losses.
- When building a shelter, the oldest snow will be the easiest to work with, since it consolidates over time.
- Snow is an excellent insulating and sound-absorbing material. From within a snow shelter, you will be unlikely to hear a search party or aircraft. You may want to make a signal above ground that can be noticed by a search party (a tarp, the word "help" or "SOS" spelled out in wood).
- In any shelter, use whatever you can find to keep yourself off the ground or snow. If pine boughs or similar soft, natural materials can be found, layer them a foot or more high, since the weight of your body will compress them considerably.
- When you are inside, the warmth from your body and your exhaled warm air will keep your shelter somewhat comfortable.

HOW TO BREAK A TRAIL IN WAIST-DEEP SNOW

⭐ **Read the terrain before choosing a route.**
In the mountains, perfectly flat expanses of snow can indicate a body of water underneath. Where possible, follow a path made up of slight inclines next to steeper slopes, to minimize the possibility of traversing incompletely frozen ponds or lakes. Never walk within 5 feet of a precipice, as snow can drift to form unstable cornices that overhang solid ground by several feet.

⭐ **Favor hard snow.**
Hard snow tends to be shiny, with light reflecting off its upper crust. It will bear your weight better than soft, powdery snow.

⭐ **Make your footprint bigger to minimize sinking.**
Wear snowshoes or wrap rags and bundles of sticks around your legs. If you don't have snowshoes and cannot locate natural materials to make your own, wrap your legs in extra clothes, a torn tarp, or another material that will help prevent your pants from becoming waterlogged, which would increase the potential for frostbite and hypothermia.

*Tamp the snow forcefully with your feet to make
the trail more permanent.*

✪ Use walking poles or a stick to probe the ground in front of you.
If the tips break through ice, walk backwards several paces, retracing your footsteps. Survey your surroundings, then choose another route.

✪ Take small steps.
As you progress, tamp down the snow forcefully with your feet and knees to make the trail more permanent.

✪ When in a group, walk in a single-file line.
Because breaking trail requires far more energy than walking over a firm path, share the effort by rotating the leader to the back of the line every 15 minutes. Switching frequently will minimize water lost through perspiration by any one member of the group, ultimately conserving fluids for all and preventing unwanted sweat from cooling the body too rapidly.

How to Make an Improvised Snowshoe

1 Bend a flexible sapling into a large teardrop shape.
Secure the ends to one another by lashing them with string, duct tape, or an extra bootlace.

2 Bind three sets of three sticks together.
Find sticks slightly longer than the width of the teardrop, then tape or tie them together in sets of three.

3 Lash the crossing sticks to the teardrop frame.
Situate the bundles of sticks so they are parallel to one another, making a ladder across the frame.

4 Anchor your boot into the frame.
Tie string across each shoe, securing it to each bundle of sticks where it overlaps the frame. Tie the rear line around your ankle for additional support.

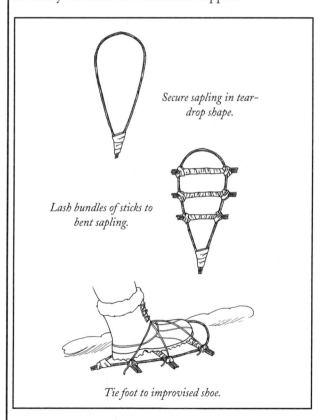

Secure sapling in tear-drop shape.

Lash bundles of sticks to bent sapling.

Tie foot to improvised shoe.

HOW TO FISH ON
THE ICE

1 | Find bait or fashion a lure.
Small fish sometimes congregate near the surface in shallow waters. If the ice is thin enough to see through, drop a heavy rock and gather the fish that have been stunned. If finding live bait is impractical, make a lure by tying feathers from a bird or a down sleeping bag to the base of a fishing hook, camouflaging its barb.

2 | Identify the best spot for catching big fish.
Large fish tend to favor deep pools. Investigate your surroundings to determine where the deep water is likely to be, such as on the outer banks of a bay. Remember that ice-fishing is like all fishing: some spots will be more productive than others for reasons that are difficult to parse.

3 | Read the ice to minimize your danger of falling through.
Dirty ice tends to be weaker than thick ice. Snow-covered ice tends to be thinner than bare ice. Always avoid rocks or other objects that protrude from the surface of the ice; underlying currents and eddies can have a warming effect. When walking on river ice, stick to the inside portion of any bends; the faster-moving water on the outside of bends makes for weaker ice.

4 Cut a hole in the thick ice.

Use a saw or a long knife to carve out a hole in the ice. Never use a naturally occurring hole, which is likely to be surrounded by dangerously thin ice. If your tools are insufficient, build a small fire to melt a hole in the ice.

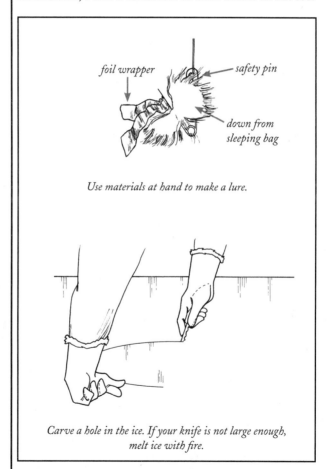

foil wrapper *safety pin*

down from sleeping bag

Use materials at hand to make a lure.

Carve a hole in the ice. If your knife is not large enough, melt ice with fire.

5 Bait your hook.

If you are using live bait, insert the hook below the dorsal fin, making a hole beneath the backbone.

6 Lower your line as deep as possible.

7 Slowly pull the line toward the surface.

Jiggle it up and down as you raise it.

8 If your hole is productive, keep it from freezing over when not in use.

Cover the hole with branches and snow. Check it routinely and chop through any new layer of ice that has formed.

Be Aware

- Make hooks of various sizes to maximize your potential catch. The sturdiest hooks are made from strips of metal or carved bone. Carved wood can also be used; season it over a flame to harden it first.
- When you catch a fish, investigate the contents of its stomach. If it contains freshly swallowed fish, save them as bait. Use partially digested food as chum, tossing it through your hole to attract more fish. Learn what the fish like to eat and try to bait your hook with similar food.

HOW TO FIND YOUR WAY WITHOUT A COMPASS

STICK AND SHADOW METHOD

Be aware that the closer you are to the equator, the less accurate this method is.

WHAT YOU NEED:
- An analog watch
- A six-inch stick

Northern Hemisphere

1 Place a small stick vertically in the ground so that it casts a shadow.

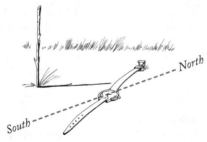

In the Northern Hemisphere, place your watch on the ground so that the hour hand is parallel to the shadow. In the Southern Hemisphere, place your watch so that 12 o'clock is parallel to the shadow.

2 | Place your watch on the ground so that the hour hand is parallel to the shadow of the stick.

3 | Find the point on the watch midway between the hour hand and 12 o'clock.
If the watch is on Daylight Savings Time—which is during most of the summer—use the midway point between the hour hand and 1 o'clock.

4 | Draw an imaginary line from that point through the center of the watch.
This imaginary line is a north-south line. The sun will be located toward the south.

Southern Hemisphere

⭐ | Place your watch on the ground so that 12 o'clock is parallel to the shadow.
Then find the midway point between the hour hand and 12 o'clock. Draw an imaginary line from the point through the center of the watch. This is the north-south line. The sun will be located toward the north.

STAR METHOD

Northern Hemisphere

⭐ | Locate the North Star, Polaris.
The North Star is the last star in the handle of the Little Dipper. Walking toward it means you are walking north. You can use the Big Dipper to find the North Star. A straight imaginary line drawn between the two stars at the end of the Big Dipper's bowl will

point to the North Star. The distance to the North Star is about five times the distance between the two "pointer" stars.

Southern Hemisphere
⭐ Find the Southern Cross.
The Southern Cross is a group of four bright stars in the shape of a cross and tilted to one side. Imagine the long axis extends in a line five times its actual length. The point where this line ends is south. If you can view the horizon, draw an imaginary line straight down to the ground to create a southern landmark.

CLOUD METHOD

⭐ Look at the clouds to determine which direction they are moving.
Generally, weather moves west to east. While this may not always be true in mountain regions, it is a good rule of thumb and may help orient you.

MOSS METHOD

⭐ Locate moss.
Mosses grow in places with lots of shade and water: areas that are cool and moist. On tree trunks, the north sides tend to be more shady and moist than the south sides, and therefore, moss usually grows on the north sides of trees. However, this method is not infallible—in many forests, both sides of a tree can be shady and moist.

HOW TO SURVIVE WHEN LOST IN THE DESERT

1 Do not panic, especially if people know where you are and when you are scheduled to return.

If you have a vehicle, stay with it—do not wander!

2 If you are on foot, try to backtrack by retracing your steps.

Always move downstream or down country. Travel along ridges instead of in washes or valleys, where it is harder for you to see and for rescuers to see you.

3 If you have completely lost your bearings, try to get to a high vista and look around.

If you are not absolutely sure you can follow your tracks or prints, stay put.

4 Build smoky fires during daylight hours (tires work well) but keep a bright fire burning at night.

If fuel is limited, keep a small kindling-fire burning and have fuel ready to burn if you spot a person or vehicle.

5 If a car or plane is passing, or if you see other people off in the distance, try to signal them with one of the following methods:

In a clearing, you can use newspaper or aluminum foil weighed down with rocks to make a large triangle; this is the international distress symbol.

- A large I indicates to rescuers that someone is injured.
- An X means you are unable to proceed.
- An F indicates you need food and water.
- Three shots from a gun is another recognized distress signal.

6 To avoid heat prostration, rest frequently.
Deserts in the United States can reach temperatures upwards of 120 degrees during the day, and shade can be scarce. In the summer, sit at least 12 inches above the ground on a stool or a branch (ground temperatures can be 30 degrees hotter than the surrounding air temperature).

7 When walking during daylight hours:
- Walk slowly to conserve energy and rest at least 10 minutes every hour.
- Drink water; don't ration it.
- Avoid talking and smoking.
- Breathe through your nose, not your mouth.
- Avoid alcohol, which dehydrates.
- Avoid eating if there is not a sufficient amount of water readily available; digestion consumes water.
- Stay in the shade and wear clothing, including a shirt, hat, and sunglasses. Clothing helps ration sweat by slowing evaporation and prolonging cooling.

- Travel in the evening, at night, or early in the day.
- In cold weather, wear layers of clothing, and make sure you and your clothes are dry.
- Watch for signs of hypothermia, which include intense shivering, muscle tensing, fatigue, poor coordination, stumbling, and blueness of the lips and fingernails. If you see these signs, get dry clothing on immediately and light a fire if possible. If not, huddle close to companions for warmth.

8 Try to find water. The best places to look are:
- The base of rock cliffs.
- In the gravel wash from mountain valleys, especially after a recent rain.
- The outside edge of a sharp bend in a dry stream-bed. Look for wet sand, then dig down three to six feet to find seeping water.
- Near green vegetation. Tree clusters and other shrubbery, such as cottonwood, sycamore, or willow trees, may indicate the presence of water.
- Animal paths and flocks of birds. Following them may lead you to water.

9 Find cactus fruit and flowers.
Split open the base of cactus stalks and chew on the pith, but don't swallow it. Carry chunks of pith to alleviate thirst while walking. Other desert plants are inedible and will make you sick.

How to Prepare

When planning a trip to a desert area that is sparsely populated, always inform someone of your destination, the duration of the trip, and its intended route. Leaving without alerting anyone and getting lost means no one will be looking for you.

If traveling by car, make sure your vehicle is in good condition, and make sure you have:

- A sound battery
- Good hoses (squeeze them: they should be firm, not soft and mushy)
- A spare tire with the proper inflation
- Spare fan belts
- Tools
- Reserve gasoline and oil
- Water (five gallons for a vehicle)

How to Drive Safely

Keep an eye on the sky. Flash floods can occur in a wash any time thunderheads are in sight, even though it may not be raining where you are. If you get caught in a dust storm while driving, get off the road immediately. Turn off your driving lights and turn on your emergency flashers. Back into the wind to reduce windshield pitting by sand particles. Before driving through washes and sandy areas, test the footing. One minute on foot may save hours of hard work and prevent a punctured oil pan.

how to survive when lost in the desert

Where to Find Water

Base of rock cliffs

Gravel wash from
mountain valleys

The outside edge of
dry streambeds

Where to Find Water

Green vegetation such as sycamore trees or other shrubbery

Cactus fruit or flowers can be eaten. Split open the base and chew on the pith.

If your vehicle breaks down, stay near it; your emergency supplies are there. Raise the hood and trunk lid to denote "help needed." A vehicle can be seen for miles, but a person is very difficult to find.

- Leave a disabled vehicle only if you are positive of the route to help.
- If stalled or lost, set signal fires. Set smoky fires in the daytime, bright ones for the night. Three fires in a triangle denotes "help needed."
- If you find a road, stay on it.

WHAT TO BRING WHEN TRAVELING BY FOOT

- Water (one gallon per person per day is adequate; two or more gallons is smarter and safer)
- A map that shows the nearest populated areas
- Waterproof matches
- A cigarette lighter or flint and steel
- A survival guide
- Strong sunscreen, a hat, warm clothes, and blankets
- A pocket knife
- A metal signaling mirror
- Iodine tablets
- A small pencil and writing materials
- A whistle (three blasts denotes "help needed")
- A canteen cup
- Aluminum foil
- A compass
- A first aid kit

How to Avoid Getting Lost

- When hiking, periodically look back in the direction from where you have come. Taking a mental picture of what it will look like when you return helps in case you become lost.
- Stay on established trails if possible and mark the trail route with blazes on trees and brush, or by making *ducques* (pronounced "ducks"), which are piles of three rocks stacked on top of one another.

Ground Signals for Passing Aircraft

Pilots can read these symbols and help accordingly.

F	Need food and water	**K**	Need to know which direction to proceed
X	Require medical assistance	**△**	Distress/Believed safe to land here
Y	Yes	**N**	No
I	Serious injury/Need doctor	**□**	Need compass and map
↑	Am traveling this way	**LL**	All is well
JL	Do not understand	**SOS**	International distress symbol

HOW TO KEEP BEVERAGES COLD IN THE DESERT

1 Dig a hole.
The hole should be deep enough that the tops of the beverages will be at least 1½ to 2 feet, and as far down as 4 to 5 feet, below the surface. At about 2 feet below ground, the temperature will be about 30°F cooler than the surface. At about 5 feet, the temperature of the earth is consistently 50 to 55°F.

2 Wrap beverages in cloth.
Insulate the beverages by wrapping them in a blanket, tarp, or extra clothing to help maintain their chill.

3 Collect two flat boards.
Ideally, each board should be a foot longer and wider than the beverages. Allowing some air around the drinks adds a layer of cooling insulation.

4 Secure the beverages between the boards.
Use duct tape or rope to fasten the beverages between the boards.

5 Tie a rope around the boards.
The rope should be at least 4 feet longer than the hole is deep. Tie one end of the rope securely around the boards. Tie a flag or a colorful piece of cloth to the

Sandwich beverages between two boards.

Lower beverages into hole.

Take careful note of the location.

boards. Tie a flag or a colorful piece of cloth to the other end of the rope.

6 Lower the beverages into the hole.

7 Fill in the hole.
Keep the flag end of the rope out of the hole so you will be able to find the spot where you buried the beverages when you're ready for a drink.

8 Tie the flag to a stick.
Raise the flag off the ground on a post or stick so it will not be buried beneath a layer of sand if the desert winds kick up. Make a mental note of other landmarks in the area, such as large rocks, cacti, or other vegetation.

Be Aware

In the extreme desert heat, conserve your energy by performing physical labor at night. If you must work in the daylight, do so in the early morning and late afternoon, when the shadows are longest and you can take best advantage of the shade they afford.

HOW TO MAKE A
BUNDLE BOW
AND ARROWS

1 Collect the sticks for your bow.

Find three sticks of uniform thickness, each between two and four feet long and preferably of a lightweight, sturdy wood like bamboo, pine, ash, willow, or elm. Consider your arm strength when choosing sticks—thicker sticks provide more resistance as you pull back the bowstring, but a thicker bow also leads to faster-flying arrows.

2 Cut the sticks to size.

Cleanly sever the ends of the sticks to make each one a different length. One stick should measure between three and four feet, another should be half as long, and the last should be three-quarters the size of the longest stick.

3 Bind the sticks together.

Lay the shortest stick next to the longest one, centering it so there is equal empty space on either side of the longer stick. Secure the two sticks together using strong adhesive tape or rope. Bind the medium-sized stick to the other two, centering it on top of the other two to produce a bow that is thickest in the middle and tapers out toward the ends. Use a pocket knife to

Bind the shorter sticks to the longer one so the thickest part of the bow is in the middle. Carve a notch at either end of the longest stick.

notch

Tie a non-slip knot at one end of the bowstring.

notch

Use duct tape to form three fins at the base of the arrow.

carve a notch about an inch from the tip on either side of the longest stick.

4 | Make a bowstring.
Select a single strong cord about as long as the bow, or braid together several lengths of strong twine, to make a bowstring that will not stretch or break when it's secured to the bow. To test the string's strength, stand on one end, hold the other in one hand, and pull; if the string stretches, braid in another strand of cord. Tie a non-slip loop knot at one end of the string. (Begin by tying a loose overhand knot 6 inches from the end of the string. Thread the end back through the center of the knot, creating a loop, and wrap it around the other side of the string four times. Pass the end back through the center of the knot.)

5 | Attach the string to the bow.
Drape the loop in the knot over the top end of the bow, letting it slip beneath the notch you have cut. Tie the other end of the string securely to the notch at the bottom end of the bow, using the standard knot you prefer. Bending the bow, slip the looped end of the string up the shaft of the bow until it settles in the upper notch. The bow should now be moderately flexed.

6 | Gather wooden shoots for your arrows.
Locate and harvest straight branches about two inches longer than the distance from the bow to the back of the bowstring when the bow is flexed. Dry them in a shelter or cave or by suspending them from a tree

branch in arid weather. (This may take several days, depending on the weather.) Whittle one end of each shoot to a sharp point.

7 Attach fletching to the arrow base.

Cut three lengths of sturdy adhesive tape about six inches long. Bend one piece of tape lengthwise so it forms the shape of a U, with the sticky side facing outward. Stick the curve of the U onto the arrow, running parallel to the shaft; each side of the U should stick up in the air. Bend the second piece of tape in the same manner, sticking it to the arrow about one-third of the distance from the first piece of tape. Fold the last length of tape in the same manner, putting it midway between the first two pieces. Ensure that the tape completely encases the shaft, then press each tape flap against the flap beside it, forming three fins. To stabilize the arrow in flight, trim the fins so they are thickest at the back end of the shaft, tapering down to nothing toward the pointed front end.

HOW TO MAKE
ANIMAL TRAPS

HOLDING TRAPS

Use a holding trap (or snare) to trap small ground animals. Holding traps capture animals but do not
kill them.

1 Procure a two-foot-long wire and a small stick.
Wire is essential—animals can bite through string and
twine.

2 Wrap one end of the wire around the stick.
Twist the stick while holding the wire on both sides
of the stick with your thumb and forefinger. You will
create a small loop around the stick while wrapping
the wire around itself.

3 Remove the stick by breaking it near the wire.
Slide the ends out. You will be left with a small loop at
one end of the wire.

4 Take the other end of the wire and pass it through
the loop.
This will make a snare loop, which becomes a snare
that will tighten as the animal struggles. The snare
loop should be about five inches in diameter.

5 | Twist and tie the end of the wire to a one-foot stake.

6 | Place the snare in an animal track or at the entrance to an animal burrow or hole.

You can also use two snares, one behind the other, to increase your odds of catching something. The struggling animal caught in one snare will likely become caught in the other.

7 | Anchor the stake in the ground.

Position the stake in an area where the animal won't see it. Mark it so that you can find it later.

8 | Check the trap only once or twice daily.

Checking the trap too often may frighten away the animals. When an animal heading for its home becomes caught in the snare, it will struggle to get away, which will tighten the wire trap.

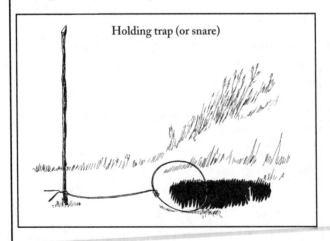

Holding trap (or snare)

Machine Traps

Machine traps use gravity, activated by a trigger, to trap or kill animals. The easiest machine trap to build is a deadfall, where a trigger releases a rock or heavy piece of wood to trap or kill an animal.

1 Look for a well-worn animal path on which to place the trap.

2 Find three straight sticks or pieces of wood that are approximately the same length and diameter, and a large, heavy stone or log.
The length and thickness of the sticks you need will depend upon the weight of the stone or log you intend to prop up—use your judgment.

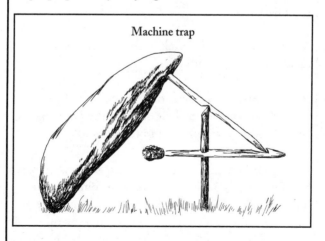

Machine trap

3 Cut a squared notch in the middle of one stick. Cut the point of the stick to look like the tip of a flat-head screwdriver—thin and flat. This is your upright support bar.

4 Cut a squared notch (to fit into the first squared notch like Lincoln Logs) in the middle of another stick. On this stick, cut a triangular notch a couple of inches from one end, and whittle the other end of the stick to a point. This is your bait bar.

5 Cut a triangular notch into the middle of the last stick. This notch should fit on the top of your support stick. Cut one point of this stick to look like the tip of a flathead screwdriver (to fit into the triangular notch of your bait bar), and cut the other end flat. This is your locking bar.

6 Anchor your support stick in the ground, perpendicular to the ground.

7 Attach a piece of meat or food to the end of your bait bar, and insert the bait bar into the notch of your support stick, parallel to the ground.

8 Place your locking bar on top of your bait and support bar, forming a 45-degree angle with your bait bar. The screwdriver tip of your locking bar should fit into the notch at the end of your bait bar, and the tip of the support bar should fit into the triangular notch of your locking bar.

9 | Lean the stone or log so that the top end rests on the top of your locking bar.

When an animal comes along the trail, it will take the bait, causing the locking bar to dislodge and trigger the deadfall, trapping or crushing your prey.

Be Aware

- To increase the odds of trapping an animal, always set multiple traps, preferably 8 to 10.
- Set the traps where animals live or in areas they frequent, near water and feeding areas. Watch animal patterns to see where they come and go regularly. Dung piles indicate nesting areas.
- Check traps once or twice daily. Dead animals will quickly rot or become food for other animals.
- Do not build the trap where you intend to place it. Build the trap components in camp, then bring them to the place you have chosen. This way, you will not frighten away animals by spending too much time in their habitats. Try to de-scent your traps using leaves or bark to remove your smell.
- Set traps in the narrow parts of animal trails, such as between rocks or in areas with thick brush on either side. Animals will generally only approach traps if there is no easy way around them. Like humans, animals tend to take the path of least resistance.
- Be careful around traps. Animal traps can injure you, and can trap bigger animals than you expect.
- Be alert when approaching any trapped animal. It may not be dead, and it may attack you.
- Do not leave traps or trap elements behind.

how to make animal traps

HOW TO CLEAN AND COOK A SQUIRREL

1   Place the squirrel on the ground, belly up.

2   Pull the end of the squirrel's tail up slightly toward you.

3   Cut.
Using a very sharp knife, make a small incision across the base of the tail, where it meets the body. Do not cut the tail completely off: The cut should be deep enough to sever the tail but should leave the skin on top of the squirrel intact.

4   Split the hide.
Make an incision through the hide down the inside of one hind leg so it connects to the cut at the tail. Repeat for the other hind leg. You should have one continuous incision from the tip of one hind leg to the tail, then back up the other hind leg.

5   Place your foot on the squirrel's tail.

6   Pull.
Pull up sharply on the squirrel's hind legs. The skin should peel off from the bottom of the squirrel to the head. Squirrels have tough skin that is difficult to remove, so it will take some time.

7 Remove the head and feet.
Cut the squirrel's head off at the neck, then cut off the feet.

8 Field dress.
Slice the belly from stem to stern and remove all entrails. Discard. Rinse off excess blood with clean water.

9 Cook.
A smaller, younger squirrel will be tender and may be roasted, while an older squirrel will have tough meat that is better stewed, if a pot is available.

To ROAST. For a youngster, sharpen a green stick (sapling) and impale the squirrel from stem to stern. Lay the sapling horizontally between two upright, forked branches positioned on either side of a fire. Slowly cook the squirrel, rotating the sapling periodically for even cooking. The meat is done when it is slightly pink inside the thickest part of the thigh. Cut with your knife to check.

To STEW. Cut an older squirrel into serving pieces: legs, back, and rib sections. Place the sections in a pot of boiling water. Add fuel to the fire to return the pot to a boil, then remove fuel as necessary to maintain a simmer. The squirrel is done when the meat falls off the bone easily. Remove from the heat and remove bones before eating.

HOW TO MAKE A FIRE FROM A SINGLE STALK OF BAMBOO

1 Split a piece of dry bamboo down the middle.
A dry bamboo stalk will be brown or tan and may have brown leaves near the top. Use a machete or sharp stone to crack it down the center. The grain of the bamboo makes it easy to split.

2 Anchor one piece of the bamboo to the ground.
Lay half the split bamboo horizontally on the ground, with the hollow side facing up. Use several wooden stakes to secure it in place.

3 Make a notch halfway down the other piece of bamboo.
Use a pocketknife to make a wedge-shaped notch that is about an inch wide on the outside of the bamboo and a narrow slit on the inside.

4 Gather several sticks of various sizes.
You will use these to feed the fire once it's started.

5 Shave thin filaments from the notched piece of bamboo.
Scrape your machete or a sharp stone back and forth over the split edges. The fine grain will peel off, forming a soft tuft of dry tinder.

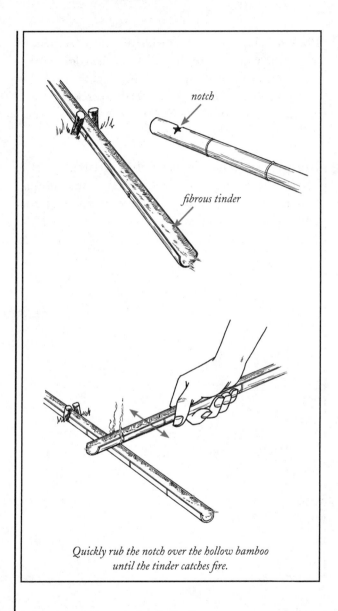

notch

fibrous tinder

*Quickly rub the notch over the hollow bamboo
until the tinder catches fire.*

6 Place the clump of tinder inside the carved notch.
Settle the wide part of the notch on the edges of the
anchored bamboo, forming an X. Rapidly drag the
top piece of bamboo back and forth to create friction
against the anchored stalk. After a while, the tinder
will begin to smoke and burn.

7 Nurse the small flame into a full-blown fire.
Place several small, dry sticks on top of the burning
tinder, gradually adding larger pieces of fuel until the
fire is of the desired size.

HOW TO MAKE FIRE WITHOUT MATCHES

- Knife
- Kindling. Several pieces, varying in size from small to large.
- Wood to keep the fire going. Select deadwood from the tree, not off the ground. Good wood should indent with pressure from a fingernail, but not break easily.
- Bow. A curved stick about two feet long.
- String. A shoelace, parachute cord, or leather thong. Primitive cordage can be made from yucca, milkweed, or another tough, stringy plant.
- Socket. A horn, bone, piece of hard wood, rock, or seashell that fits in the palm of the hand and will be placed over a stick.
- Lube. You can use earwax, skin oil, a ball of green grass, lip balm, or anything else oily.
- Spindle. A dry, straight ¾- to 1-inch-diameter stick approximately 12 to 18 inches long. Round one end and carve the other end to a point.
- Fire board. Select and shape a second piece of wood into a board approximately ¾ to 1 inch thick, 2 to 3 inches wide, and 10 to 12 inches long. Carve a shallow dish in the center of the flat side approximately ½ inch from the edge. Into the edge of this dish, cut a V-shaped notch.

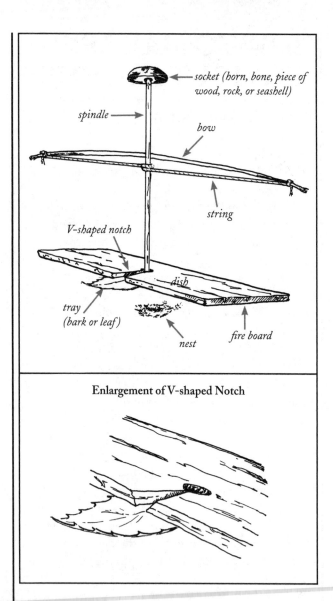

socket (horn, bone, piece of wood, rock, or seashell)

spindle

bow

string

V-shaped notch

dish

tray (bark or leaf)

nest

fire board

Enlargement of V-shaped Notch

• Tray. A piece of bark or leaf inserted under the V-shaped notch to catch the ember. The tray should not be made of deadwood.
• Nest. Dry bark, grass, leaves, cattail fuzz, or some other combustible material, formed into a bird nest shape.

HOW TO START THE FIRE

1 Tie the string tightly to the bow, one end to each end of the stick.

2 Kneel on your right knee, with the ball of your left foot on the fire board, holding it firmly to the ground.

3 Take the bow in your hands.

4 Loop the string in the center of the bow.

5 Insert the spindle in the loop of the bowstring so that the spindle is on the outside of the bow, pointed end up.
The bowstring should now be tight—if not, loop the string around the spindle a few more times.

6 Take the hand socket in your left hand, notch side down. Lubricate the notch.

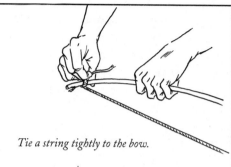

Tie a string tightly to the bow.

Loop the string in the center and insert the spindle.

Press down lightly on the socket. Draw bow back and forth, rotating spindle. Add pressure to the socket and speed your bowing motion until fire ember is produced.

7 Place the rounded end of the spindle into the dish of the fire board and the pointed end of the spindle into the hand socket.

8 Pressing down lightly on the socket, draw the bow back and forth, rotating the spindle slowly.

9 Add pressure to the socket and speed to your bowing until you begin to produce smoke and ash.
When there is a lot of smoke, you have created a fire ember.

10 Immediately stop your bowing motion and tap the spindle on the fire board to knock the ember into the tray.

11 Remove the tray and transfer the ember into your "nest."

12 Hold the nest tightly and blow steadily onto the ember. Eventually, the nest will catch fire.

13 Add kindling onto the nest. When the kindling catches, gradually add larger pieces of fuel.

Be Aware

You should not be dependent on any primitive fire method to maintain life in a wilderness survival emergency. Making fire in this manner can be quite difficult under actual harsh conditions (rain, snow, cold).

You should practice this method at home before you attempt it in the wilderness to familiarize yourself with the quirks of the process.

BEST FIREWOODS

Species	Heat per Cord (million BTUs)	Smoke	Sparks	Ease of Burning	Ease of Splitting
Apple	26–27	Minimal	Few	Poor	Easy
Oak	24–27	Minimal	Few	Poor	Hard
Beech	24–27	Minimal	Few	Poor	Easy
Birch	20–26	Minimal	Moderate	Good	Easy
Ash	19–24	Minimal	Few	Fair	Easy
Elm	19–20	Some	Few	Fair	Hard
Maple	18–19	Minimal	Few	Good	Hard
Aspen	15	Some	Few	Fair	Easy
Pine	14–15	Some	Moderate	Poor	Easy
Cedar	12–13	Some	Many	Fair	Easy

NOTE: Do not burn poison oak, poison ivy, or wood from or covered in any plants that are known to cause skin irritation. The allergy-spurring oils are most concentrated on the stems, and inhaling them through smoke may provoke respiratory problems.

HOW TO MAKE, AND COOK WITH, A PIT OVEN

1 Dig a hole.
In firm terrain, preferably in a natural depression, make a pit about three feet deep and three feet wide.

2 Cover the bottom of the hole with rocks.
Search for stones as big as grapefruits, and preferably flat. Lay them out in a solid layer. Set several rocks aside for later use.

3 Build a fire.
Collect wood and set it alight on top of the rocks in the bottom of the pit. Do not lean over the hole as the fire grows; the rocks may shoot out splinters as they heat up.

4 Spread the coals.
Using a thick branch or another long tool, scatter the burning coals evenly across the bottom of the pit.

5 Use more rocks to form a grate.
Arrange several large rocks in a square in the center of the coals.

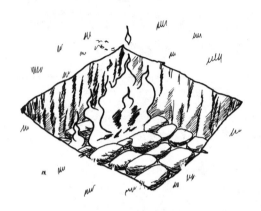

Build a fire on top of flat rocks in pit.

Spread coals, form a grate with more rocks,
and roast meat on spit.

6 Cook your food on the grate.
To cook a lizard, make a cut from shoulder to shoulder and discard the head and neck; peel the skin off after cooking is complete. For rodents, use a knife to remove all hair and skin before cooking, as well as abdominal organs such as the stomach and intestines. Younger animals are more tender and therefore can be skewered on a stick and roasted; older animals will be better when stewed in boiling water. Drink the cooking water for additional nutrients.

7 Seal in the heat.
To make the meat cook faster, lay a dampened canvas tarp on top of the pit to trap the heat inside the oven. Set rocks around the perimeter of the tarp to keep it in place.

8 Cover the pit with sand when you are finished.
Shovel a pile of sand into the pit to cover the hot rocks before you leave the area.

UNIVERSAL EDIBILITY TEST

1. Abstain from eating for 8 hours before testing a new possible food source.

2. Separate the plant into its basic components: seeds, leaves, stems, flowers, buds, and roots.

3. Test for contact poisoning by placing the plant part in the crook of your elbow for 15 minutes. If no irritation follows, proceed.

4. Place the plant part on your lips for 3 minutes to make sure it won't cause a burning or itching sensation.

5. Place the plant part on your tongue for 15 minutes to make sure it causes no irritation.

6. If there has been no adverse reaction, chew a small portion and hold it in your mouth for 15 minutes.

7. If no irritation or numbness results, swallow the small plant morsel.

8. Abstain from eating anything else for 8 hours. If vomiting or nausea ensues, drink plenty of water to flush out your system. If there are no adverse effects, prepare a small handful of the plant part and eat the whole portion. If another 8 hours pass without irritation or vomiting, consider the plant safe to eat.

HOW TO SURVIVE ADRIFT AT SEA

1 Stay aboard your boat as long as possible before you get into a life raft.

In a maritime emergency, the rule of thumb is that you should step up into your raft, meaning you should be up to your waist in water before you get into the raft. Your best chance of survival is on a boat—even a disabled one—not on a life raft. But if the boat is sinking, know how to use a life raft. Any craft that sails in open water (a boat larger than 14 feet) should have at least one life raft. Smaller boats may only have life jackets, so these vessels should stay within easy swimming distance of land.

2 Get in the life raft, and take whatever supplies you can carry.

Most importantly, if you have water in jugs, take it with you. Do not drink seawater. A person can last for several days without food at sea, but without clean water to drink, death is a virtual certainty within several days. If worse comes to worst, throw the jugs of water overboard so that you can get them later—they will float.

Many canned foods, particularly vegetables, are packed in water, so take those with you if you can. Do not ration water; drink it as needed, but don't drink more than is necessary—a ½-gallon a day should be sufficient if you limit your activity.

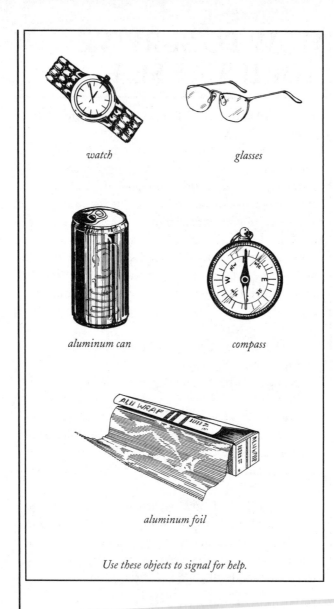

watch

glasses

aluminum can

compass

aluminum foil

Use these objects to signal for help.

3 | **Remain in the vicinity of the ship you've abandoned.**
Rescuers answering an SOS message have the best chance of finding you if you stay close to your starting coordinates. Construct a makeshift sea anchor by tying a rope around the handle of a bucket or a roll of expendable clothing and secure the other end of the rope to the raft. Put the anchor in the water on the windward side to keep the front of the boat facing into the wind, making the raft less likely to capsize and minimizing the amount of drift caused by wind.

4 | **If you are in a cold water/weather environment, get warm.**
You are more likely to die of exposure or hypothermia than of anything else. Put on dry clothes and stay out of the water; prolonged exposure to saltwater can damage your skin and cause lesions, which are prone to infection. Stay covered. Modern life rafts have canopies, which protect passengers from sun, wind, and rain. If the canopy is missing or damaged, wear a hat, long sleeves, and pants to protect yourself from the sun.

5 | **Find food, if you can.**
Life rafts include fishing hooks in their survival kits. If your raft is floating for several weeks, seaweed will form on its underside and fish will naturally congregate in the shade under you. You can catch them with the hook and eat the flesh raw. If no hook is available, you can fashion one using wire or even shards of aluminum from an empty can.

6 Use the wind to your advantage.
If you were not able to issue a distress call before you abandoned ship and you do not believe that help is on the way, improvise a sail. Tie two paddles securely to opposite sides of the raft. Stretch a sheet or poncho between the upright paddles. Use a third paddle as a rudder.

7 Read the clouds for signs of land.
Dense, puffy clouds with a flat bottom (cumulus clouds) in an otherwise clear sky usually form over land. White, fluffy clouds indicate good weather. A darker color spells rain. A greenish tint is known as "lagoon glare," which results from sunlight reflecting off shallow water, where it may be easiest to catch fish.

8 Let animals be your guides.
Seals in water are a guarantee that land is nearby, since they rarely venture far from shore. Single sea birds often leave land far behind, but flocks of birds are almost never more than 60 miles from the shore. They fly out to sea in the morning and return in the late afternoon to roost. Base your direction of travel on the time of day, heading in the opposite direction of the birds' flight in the morning and following them to shore in the evening.

9 Try to get to land, if you know where it is.
Most rafts include small paddles, but life rafts are not very maneuverable, especially in any wind above three

knots. Do not exhaust yourself—you will not be able to move any significant distance without great effort.

10 **If you see a plane or boat nearby, try to signal them.** Use a VHF radio or a handheld flare kit to get their attention. A small mirror can also be used for signaling.

Improvise a sail and use a paddle as a rudder.

To bounce sunlight off a small mirror or wristwatch dial to signal a passing aircraft, hold one hand at arm's length from your face with two fingers spread into a V. Use your other hand to position your mirror just under one eye, facing away from you, and frame the helicopter or airplane between your two raised fingers. Swivel the mirror back and forth so that the reflected light jumps from one finger to another—as you do so, the light will hit the plane in the middle.

Be Aware

- Do not drink saltwater directly from the ocean, no matter how thirsty you feel. Spread a tarp for collecting rainwater and dew. If the tarp is coated with dried salt, wash it off in seawater before spreading it; there will not be enough salt introduced by rinsing the tarp in seawater to harm you. Drink as much rainwater as you can to remain hydrated, especially when your freshwater supply is limited.

- Sunburn is a serious concern while afloat in the sea. If your life raft does not already have a roof, rig one using whatever material you have available and cover all exposed skin. Your face and neck are especially vulnerable and in need of protection.

- If you see sharks in the water near you, remain still and quiet. Do not put any body parts or equipment in the water. If you have a fish on the line when you spot a shark, let the fish go. Do not gut fish into the water when sharks are near.

HOW TO SURVIVE
WHEN MAROONED

⭐ Find drinkable water.
Gather rainwater by hollowing out the stumps of trees,
but do not let the water sit for more than a day before
drinking it. Tie rags around your ankles and walk
through grass at dawn, then squeeze the dew from the
rags into your mouth. The water in coconuts is safe to
drink, though excessive consumption may cause diar-
rhea and dehydration. An island that appears to be
dry may have a wet, mountainous interior, so move to
higher ground to survey as much of the terrain as possible. In arctic environments, search for blue ice with
round corners and that splinters easily—this is old sea
ice and is nearly free of salt. Icebergs are also made of
freshwater. If you are desperate, drink the water found
in the eyes and spines of large fish.

⭐ Take care of your body.
Stay in the shade to protect yourself from the sun as
well as from the reflection of the sun on the water. If
you are in a tropical environment, dampen your clothes
on the hottest part of the day to cool yourself and to
avoid losing water through perspiration. If fresh water
is readily available, use this water to moisten your
clothes to avoid the boils and sores caused by saltwater. If you are in an arctic environment, find a cave or
dig yourself a shelter in the snow to keep your body
temperature up. Relax and sleep when possible.

how to survive when marooned

Tie shirt securely around a forked branch.

Scoop fish from underneath to catch.

★ **Find food.**
Make a fish net by placing your shirt over a forked tree branch and tying off both ends. Pull fish out of shallow water as they swim over the net. Fish without spiny scales may be eaten raw or cooked. Kill seabirds by throwing rocks at them, as long as you have fire to cook them. You may be able to attract birds by flashing metal into the sky to get their attention. Do not eat anything if you are nauseated; drink only water and wait to eat until your stomach is calm.

★ **Signal.**
Make a signal fire by quickly rotating a small stick back and forth between your palms while one end is pressed against a piece of flat wood on the ground. The friction will create heat, which will ignite dry grass. Keep a small fire burning at all times, with plenty of fuel ready in case you spot a passing ship.

★ **Keep a good lookout.**
Chances are your ship was sailing on a known trade route, and other ships are likely to sail within several miles of your island. Move to high ground so you can see the horizon in every direction.

FIVE CRITICAL KNOTS

FIGURE 8

Used to keep the end of a rope from running out, as through a pulley on a boat.

BOWLINE

Used to make a small, nonslipping loop to secure around an object.

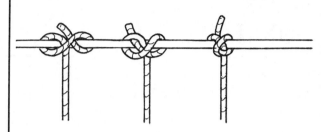

CONSTRICTOR
Used for securing a load. May be difficult to untie when pulled tight.

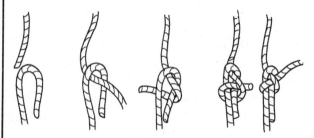

SHEET BEND
Typically used to join two ropes together.

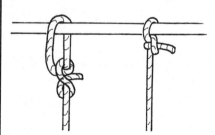

TWO HALF HITCHES
Used in mooring a boat.

HOW TO
PURIFY WATER

There are four ways to obtain safe drinking water in the wilderness: filtration, chemical treatment, boiling, and distillation.

FILTRATION

Filter water from all sources in the wild—mountain stream, spring, river, lake, or pond.

1 Find or make your filter.
Coffee filters, paper towels, ordinary typing paper, or even your clothing can serve as filters (the more tightly woven, the better). You can also make an effective filter by filling a sock with alternating layers of crushed charcoal, small crushed rocks, and sand.

2 Pour the water through a filter.
Do this several times to clean out impurities.

Be Aware
Filtration will only remove some of the water's impurities. It will not kill bacteria or other microorganisms. The best procedure is to filter water first, then treat it with chemicals or boil it.

Chemical Treatment

1 Add two drops of household bleach for each quart of water.
Use three drops if the water is extremely cold or cloudy.

Or

Use one iodine tablet or five drops of drugstore iodine (2 percent) per quart of water.

2 Mix the water and bleach or iodine, and let it sit for at least one hour.
The chemicals will kill microorganisms; the longer the water sits, the purer it will be. Leaving the water overnight is the safest course of action.

Distillation

A solar still uses the heat of the sun to evaporate water trapped in the ground and funnels it into a container for drinking. To build a solar still:

1 Dig a hole about a foot deep, and wide enough to hold your container.

2 Place a clean container at the center of the hole.

3 Cover the hole with a piece of plastic.
A tarp or a section of a garbage bag works well as a cover.

4 Place sticks or stones around the edges of the plastic so that it is flush with the ground and air cannot escape.

5 Poke a ¼- to ½-inch hole in the center of the tarp and place a small stone next to the hole, so the tarp looks like a funnel.
Make sure the hole is above, but not touching, the top of the container.

6 Wait.
The heat from the sun will cause water in the ground to evaporate, condense on the plastic, and drip into the container. While your solar still will not produce much liquid (less than one cup), the water is safe to drink immediately. The process can take anywhere from several hours to a full day to produce water, depending on the water in the ground and the strength of the sun.

BOILING

★ Boil water for at least one minute, plus one minute of boiling time for each 1,000 feet above sea level.
If fuel is abundant, boil water for 10 minutes before drinking it. The longer the water boils, the more microorganisms that are killed. Beyond 10 minutes, however, no further purification occurs. Be sure to let the water cool before drinking it.

HOW TO BUILD A JUNGLE SHELTER

1 Clear the vegetation from a flat, dry area.

The space for your shelter need only be slightly longer than your body, and about twice the width. Avoid areas where signs of erosion indicate a danger of flash floods.

2 Drive four posts into the ground, one at each corner of the area.

Collect four logs or branches about as tall as your shoulder and about six inches across. Use a sharpened stick to dig the post holes, then pound a post into each hole to a depth of at least one foot, so the pole stands as tall as your waist.

3 Carve a notch on each pole.

Use a pocketknife or a sharp stick to carve a two-inch notch into the outward face of each pole, at a uniform height just below knee-level.

4 Collect materials for the frame of the structure.

Find six straight sapling trunks or sturdy tree branches about four inches in diameter, or thick enough to hold your weight. You'll need two saplings about two feet longer than the width of your shelter area (probably between five and seven feet long) and four more saplings about two feet longer than the length of your shelter (about nine feet long).

how to build a jungle shelter

apex

gable

2 feet

*Sleep about two feet off the ground to protect yourself
from flash floods, insects, fungal infections, hypothermia,
and wild animal attacks.*

5 Create the frame at the head and foot of the shelter.
Form a horizontal bar by placing the ends of one of
the shorter saplings into the notches in the poles at the
head of the shelter. Repeat at the foot of the shelter.
Secure both saplings to the poles with rope or vines.
Ideally, the ends of both crossbars should protrude
about one foot beyond the posts they're resting on.

6 Create the frame for the sides of the shelter.
Use two of the long remaining saplings to form the crossbars for the sides, laying them on top of the protruding ends of the crossbars at the shelter's top and bottom. Lash them in place with ropes or vines.

7 Make a bed from sturdy, smaller branches.
Gather several dozens of straight branches about two inches in diameter and about two feet longer than the width of the shelter frame. Place them so that they span from one side of the frame to the other, and lash them in place with ropes or vines.

8 Collect materials to make the roof.
Find five straight branches or saplings measuring about two inches in diameter: one should be two feet longer than the length of the shelter (this will form the apex), and the other four should be two feet longer than the width of the shelter (these will form the gables).

9 Make the frame for the roof.
Carve a two-inch notch into the outward face of each upright pole an inch or two from the top. Lay the two remaining long and thick saplings gathered in step 4 into the notches to create another pair of lengthwise crossbars at the top of the shelter. Lash a pair of gable branches together at one end, creating a right angle between them; then lash the free ends to the top of the head posts. Repeat with the other gable branches at the foot of the shelter. Finally, lash the

long apex sapling into the V shape at the top of each gable, creating a lengthwise crossbar for your roof.

10 Finish the roof.
Fill in the frame by lashing branches that run horizontally from one end of the shelter to the other. These branches should be about an inch thick, or sturdy enough to support heavy leaves. Drape large leaves over the roof frame, overlapping them from top to bottom to form natural shingles.

Be Aware
An elevated shelter is essential in tropical environments. Sleeping directly on the ground may lead to fungal infections; leech infestation; attacks from wild boars, snakes, and other large animals; hypothermia; or drowning by flash flood.

SAFELY ORDER WHEN YOU DON'T SPEAK THE LANGUAGE

Point to any item(s) you wish to order. Point to slash-through and any item you do not wish to order.

NO

mushrooms

chicken

garlic

fish

tomato

pork

chile peppers

onion

goat

broccoli

beef

wine

beer

bottled water

coffee

tap water

tea

iced water

noodles

shrimp

egg

toast

fruit

pizza

hamburger

french fries

HOW TO PASS
A BRIBE

1 If you are hassled by an official, be friendly, but aloof. Do not show concern or act surly. Remain calm and good-natured. Try to determine if there is an actual problem or if the official is seeking some additional, unofficial compensation.

2 Never blatantly offer a bribe.
If you have misinterpreted the official's intentions, you may get yourself in additional trouble by overtly offering a bribe.

3 If you are accused of an infraction, ask to pay a fine on the spot.
Say that you would rather not deal with the mail or go to another location, citing your fear that the payment will get lost. Mention that you want to make sure the money gets to the proper person.

4 Try to speak to and deal with only one official.
Speak to the person who acts as though he/she is in charge. If you offer money to a junior officer while a superior is present, the superior may demand more.

5 Offer to make a "donation" to the official's organization.
Say that you would like to pay for gas, uniforms, car repairs, expenses, or other needs.

To resolve a customs dispute, offer the official a "sample" of the goods in question—for example, a bottle of liquor.

6 | If you do not have cash, be prepared to offer goods instead.

Watches, cameras, and other electronics are often accepted as bribes. You might consider offering goods instead of cash even if you have the money, particularly if the "problem" concerns these goods. If, for example, a customs official tells you that you are transporting too many bottles of liquor, you might speed your trip and lighten your load by offering some of the items in dispute to the official.

Be Aware

Carry only a small amount of money in your wallet and hide the rest. This will prevent an unscrupulous official from seeing your entire wad.

HOW TO SURVIVE A NIGHT IN JAIL

1 Request a single.

If you notice an empty cell, ask to be housed there. Do not offer special reasons for wanting a private cell—those factors may work against you if you are later placed in a group cell.

2 Do not show fear.

Fear means weakness in jail. If you cannot stop shaking, pretend you are psychologically unsound: Wave your arms around, babble nonsense, and yell at no one in particular.

Relax hand and roll finger to make a clean print.

3 | Stay within sight of the guard.
The cell may be monitored in person by a guard or via closed-circuit television. Make sure you remain visible.

4 | Do not sleep.
Lying down on a bench or cot gives other inmates the opportunity to claim that you are lying on "their" bunk. Sit on the floor with your back to the wall, preferably in a corner of the cell. Do not remove any clothing to use as a blanket or pillow, or you will risk losing the item to other inmates.

5 | Keep to yourself.
Do not start a conversation with anyone, but do not be rude. Answer any questions you are asked, and keep your responses short. Do not talk about the reason for your arrest, as there may be police informants in the cell. Do not make eye contact with other inmates, but do not avert your eyes.

6 | Do not accept favors.
Other inmates may offer to help you in various ways, then claim that you "owe" them. Resist the temptation to ask for or accept help.

7 | Do not try to escape.

HOW TO
TAIL A THIEF

1 Before attempting to follow someone who
you believe has stolen from you, try to alter
your appearance.
Remove your jacket, if you were wearing one; remove
your shirt, if you are wearing a T-shirt underneath; put
on or remove a hat or sunglasses. You do not want the
thief to recognize you.

2 Never stare directly at the person you are following.
You can observe the person without being obvious.
Never make eye contact.

3 Note the thief's identifying characteristics (dress,
gait, height, and weight).
You will be able to keep track of the thief in a crowd
(or after losing sight of him or her) if you are looking
for particular details.

4 Stay well behind the person you are following.
Never tail a person by walking right behind him or
her. Follow from a distance of at least 40 feet, or from
across the street.

5 If the thief goes into a store, do not follow.
Remain outside, looking in the store window, or wait a
few doors down for the thief to come out. If the thief
does not emerge quickly, check for a back exit.

6 Once you have determined that the thief has arrived at his or her destination, call the authorities. Confronting thieves alone is risky. Use a phone or ask a storeowner to call the police. Describe your target and his or her location.

Be Aware

Wallet thieves and pickpockets often follow a similar pattern: They pass the wallet to another person immediately following the theft in order to throw you off the trail, and that person passes it to another. If you can, follow the initial thief: The thief may no longer be carrying your wallet, but might lead you to those who are.

HOW TO TREAT A BULLET OR KNIFE WOUND

1 Do not immediately pull out any impaled objects.
Bullets, arrows, knives, sticks, and the like cause penetrating injuries. When these objects lodge in the vital areas of the body (the trunk or near nerves or arteries) removing them may cause more severe bleeding that cannot be controlled. The object may be pressed against an artery or other vital internal structure and may actually be helping to reduce the bleeding.

2 Control the bleeding by using a combination of direct pressure, limb elevation, pressure points, and tourniquets (in that order).

DIRECT PRESSURE. You can control most bleeding by placing direct pressure on the wound. Attempt to apply pressure directly to bleeding surfaces. The scalp, for instance, bleeds profusely. Using your fingertips to press the edges of a scalp wound against the underlying bone is more effective than using the palm of your hand to apply pressure over a wider area. Use the tips of your fingers to control bleeding arterioles (small squirting vessels).

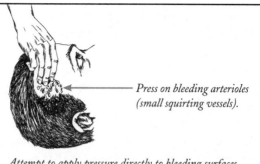

Press on bleeding arterioles
(small squirting vessels).

*Attempt to apply pressure directly to bleeding surfaces.
Using fingertips rather than the palm is more effective
for scalp wounds. Attempt to promote clotting.*

*If injury is in a limb, use pressure to control bleeding, and
elevate limb. Dress the wound to prevent spread of infection.*

LIMB ELEVATION. When a wound is in an extremity, elevation of the extremity above the heart, in addition to direct pressure, may reduce the bleeding further. Never make people who are in shock sit up simply to elevate a bleeding wound.

PRESSURE POINTS. To reduce blood flow you usually have to compress an artery (where you can feel the pulse) near the wound against an underlying bone. Just pressing into the soft belly of a muscle does not reduce blood flow by this mechanism.

TOURNIQUETS. A tourniquet is a wide band of cloth or a belt that is placed around an extremity and tightened (usually using a windlass) until the blood flow is cut off. The blood supply must be compressed against a long bone (the upper arm or upper leg) since vessels between the double bones in the lower arm and lower leg will continue to bleed despite a tourniquet. The amount of pressure necessary typically causes additional vascular and nerve trauma that is permanent. A tourniquet should only be used as a last resort—to save a life at the expense of sacrificing a limb.

3 Immobilize the injured area.
Using splints and dressings to immobilize an injured area helps protect from further injury and maintain clots that have begun to form. Even if an injury to a bone or joint is not suspected, immobilization will promote clotting and help healing begin.

4 Dress the wound, and strive to prevent infection.
Use sterile (or at least clean) dressings as much as possible. Penetrating injuries may allow anaerobic (air-hating) bacteria to get deep into the tissue. This is why penetrating wounds are typically irrigated with sterile or antibiotic solutions in surgery. While this is rarely practical outside of the hospital, it is important to remember that smaller penetrating wounds (nail holes in the foot and the like) should be encouraged to bleed for a short period to help "wash out" foreign material. Soaking an extremity in hydrogen peroxide may help kill anaerobic bacteria as well. Do not apply

ointments or goo to penetrating wounds as these may actually promote infection.

Emergency Tip
Some data indicate that pure granular sugar poured into a penetrating wound can decrease bleeding, promote clotting, and discourage bacteria. You are not likely to see it used in your local emergency department, but it might be worth consideration if your circumstances are dire.

5 Get medical attention as soon as possible.

Be Aware
It should be noted that tourniquets are rarely helpful—it is uncommon to have life-threatening bleeding in an extremity that cannot be controlled by the methods described above. The areas that cause fatal bleeding (like the femoral arteries or intra-abdominal bleeding) do not lend themselves to the use of a tourniquet. Even most complete amputations do not bleed all that much, and are controlled by direct pressure. Arteries that are severed only part of the way through tend to bleed more profusely than those that are completely severed.

How to Take a Bullet

1 Face the shooter.
You do not want to take the bullet in your back or the base of your skull.

how to treat a bullet or knife wound

2 | Get low.
In addition to making yourself a smaller target, by keeping a low profile you will be better able to protect your head, neck, and midline—all areas where a bullet wound is most likely to cause fatal injury or permanent disability.

3 | Sit.
Sit with your rear end on the ground. Bend your knees and keep your legs in front of you, protecting your midline with your shins and thighs.

4 | Move your elbows into the center of your body.
Place both forearms in front of you, covering your face.

5 | Place your hands over your head.
Hold your fingers together, with your palms toward you. Keep your hands an inch or two in front of you to absorb the impact of the bullet.

6 | Wait for the impact.
You may notice little more than a "punch" sensation, or you may feel nothing at all.

7 | Determine the site of the injury.
Bullet wounds in the hands and feet, lower legs, and forearms are rarely fatal, provided blood loss is controlled.

8 Control the bleeding.
Place firm, direct pressure on the wound to slow blood loss. If the bullet entered an appendage and pressure does not stop the bleeding, use a belt or narrow strip of cloth as a tourniquet. Place the tourniquet on the affected limb, several inches above the injury site. It should be tight enough to stop heavy blood flow. A tourniquet may cause permanent damage to the affected limb, and should be used only as a last resort. Never leave a tourniquet in place for more than a few minutes.

9 Get help.
Seek medical attention as soon as possible.

Be Aware
- If you are crouching next to a wall, stay a foot or more away from the surface. Bullets will skid along the wall after impact.
- Gunshot wounds to the neck are almost always fatal.
- Most interior walls and doors (including car doors) will not stop a bullet larger than .22 or .25 caliber.

Glossary of Manly Terms

Beer: Ancient beverage, made from fermented starches, and the third most widely consumed drink in the world. It is delicious.

Boxing: Sport in which two people hit each other until one of them falls down and is unable to get up.

Bromance: Kind and loving behavior toward a male friend, including eating, drinking, and watching movies together; accompanying each other on outings; and trips to Las Vegas, but never gets to first base. See also: Romance.

Capsaicin: Magic chemical that gives peppers their heat, allowing for the production of hot sauce—the application of which improves the taste of any food item.

Cat: Domesticated mammal of the *Felis* family. Something for your dog to run after.

Chainsaw: Motorized saw, with a drive mechanism attached to a saw chain threaded around a channel. Used to cut down trees or scare the neighbor's kids off the lawn.

Chore: Small household task, such as doing dishes or folding laundry, often assigned by one's spouse or partner, best put off or avoided altogether.

Dieting: Limiting consumption of donuts, bacon, and cheeseburgers to one serving per day.

Dog: Domesticated mammal of the *Canidae* family, of the order *Carnivore*. Your best friend.

Football: Competitive team sport in which goals are scored by carrying or throwing an ovoid ball into the opposing team's end zone; best enjoyed while eating potato chips and drinking alcohol.

Golf: Three hours of people wandering around in ridiculous outfits. An ideal way to spend an afternoon.

Grill: Cooking machine located in the outdoors, allowing user to closely replicate sensation of a caveman cooking mastodon meat over a fire pit.

Hammer: Heavy tool with a long handle, useful for driving nails into walls, clawing out nails that you drove in mistakenly, and dropping on your feet and cursing.

Horsepower: Unit of power, equal to 746 watts, used to measure the output of car engines, and, correlatively, manhood.

Lawnmower: Machine with revolving blades for cutting a lawn. See if you can get the neighbor's kid to use it to trim your grass.

Masturbation: The imagined physical and romantic conjoining of a man and a girl he sort of remembers from college.

Necktie: Piece of colored fabric worn around the neck, often used to tie men to desk jobs.

Pornography: Material causing a heightened physiognomic response, such as pictures of naked women or a rib eye steak.

Power drill: Like a screwdriver, except it plugs in or is battery operated, can just make holes in things as well as screw in screws, and is awesome.

Riding mower: Machine with revolving blades for cutting a lawn. It is also awesome.

Romance: Kind and loving behavior towards your spouse or partner, such as bringing home flowers, remembering her birthday, and saying "excuse me" when farting during dinner. See also: Bromance.

Screwdriver: Metal device with a plastic handle, having a number of different heads (Phillips-head, flat-head, etc.) for the insertion and tightening of screws or making of holes. Also a delicious and refreshing beverage made of vodka and orange juice in a proportion of 2 to 5, served over ice.

Sex: The physical and romantic conjoining of a man and a woman for the purposes of reproduction and/or recreation; subject of near-constant thought.

Sledge hammer: A really big hammer.

Soccer: Competitive team sport in which goals are scored by kicking a spherical ball into the opposing goal; widely enjoyed by Europeans (who call it "football" for some reason) and third graders.

Television: Magical device for receiving broadcast images, which upon its invention in the 1920s swiftly supplanted books and the spoken word as mankind's best means of communication.

Testosterone: Hormone produced by the testes and responsible equally for every cool or dumb idea you ever have.

Whiskey: Alcoholic liquor distilled from grain and aged in wooden container, made anywhere but Scotland.

Whisky: Whiskey made in Scotland.

Wine: Ancient beverage, made from fermented grapes, to be drunk in emergencies when beer is unavailable.

Wrestling: Sport in which two people pick each other up and throw each other around until one of them is unable to get up.

ABOUT THE AUTHORS

David Borgenicht is a writer and publisher who lives with his family in Philadelphia. He is the coauthor of all the books in the *Worst-Case Scenario Survival Handbook* series.

Brenda Brown is an illustrator and cartoonist whose work has been published in many books and publications, including *The Worst-Case Scenario* series, *Esquire*, *Reader's Digest*, *USA Weekend*, *21st Century Science & Technology*, the *Saturday Evening Post*, and the *National Enquirer*. Her website is www.webtoon.com.

Jim Grace is coauthor of *The Worst-Case Scenario Survival Handbook: Golf*.

Sarah Jordan is coauthor of *The Worst-Case Scenario Survival Handbook: Parenting* and *The Worst-Case Scenario Survival Handbook: Weddings*.

Piers Marchant is coauthor of *The Worst-Case Scenario Survival Handbook: Life* and *The Worst-Case Scenario Almanac: History*.

Joshua Piven is the coauthor, along with David Borgenicht, of all the *Worst-Case Scenario Survival Handbooks*. He lives in Philadelphia with his family.

Dan and Judy Ramsey are coauthors of *The Worst-Case Scenario Pocket Guide: Retirement*.

Victoria De Silverio is coauthor of *The Worst-Case Scenario Pocket Guide: Breakups*.

Sam Stall is coauthor of *The Worst-Case Scenario Pocket Guide: Dogs*.

Ben H. Winters is coauthor of *The Worst-Case Scenario Pocket Guides* for *Cars*, *Cats*, *Meetings*, *New York City*, and *San Francisco*.

Jennifer Worick is coauthor of *The Worst-Case Scenario Survival Handbook: College* and *The Worst-Case Scenario Survival Handbook: Dating & Sex*.

THE FIRST OF THE WORST

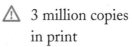 3 million copies in print

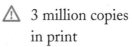 Translated into 27 languages

 International best-seller

"An armchair guide for the anxious."
—*USA Today*

"The book to have when the killer bees arrive."
—*The New Yorker*

"Nearly 180 pages of immediate action drills for when everything goes to hell in a handbasket."
—*Soldier of Fortune*

"This is a really nifty book."
—*Forbes*

A BOOK FOR EVERY DISASTER

HANDBOOKS

Original

Travel

Dating & Sex

Golf

Holidays

Work

College

Weddings

Parenting

Extreme Edition

Life

Almanacs

History

Great Outdoors

Politics

Pocket Guides

Dogs

Cats

New York City

San Francisco

Retirement

Breakups

Meetings

Cars

Also Available

- *The Complete Worst-Case Scenario Survival Handbook*
- *The Worst-Case Scenario Book of Survival Questions*
- *The Worst-Case Scenario Daily Survival Calendar*

MORE WORST-CASE SCENARIOS

Visit our partners' websites for more Worst-Case
Scenario products:

⭐ **Board games**

www.universitygames.com

⭐ **Mobile**

www.namcogames.com

⭐ **Posters and puzzles**

www.aquariusimages.com/wcs.html

For updates, new scenarios, and more, visit: www.worstcasescenarios.com

To order books visit: www.chroniclebooks.com/worstcase

Because you just never know . . . .